THE CONFIDENT COACH'S GUIDE
TO TEACHING YOUTH SOCCER

THE CONFIDENT COACH'S GUIDE TO TEACHING YOUTH SOCCER

From Basic Fundamentals to Advanced Player Skills and Team Strategies

Joe Provey

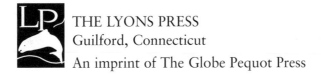

THE LYONS PRESS
Guilford, Connecticut
An imprint of The Globe Pequot Press

To my children,
Joseph, Renald, and Corinna—
who put up with me as their
coach for so many years.

————————

The Lyons Press is an imprint of The Globe Pequot Press.

10 9 8 7 6 5 4 3 2 1

Printed in the United States of America

ISBN 1-59228-808-1

Library of Congress Cataloging-in-Publication Data is available on file.

CONTENTS

FOREWORD

My high school soccer coach, rest his soul, had been an all-state catcher during his playing days. When I met him, he was a gentle bear of a man who liked kids, but what he knew about soccer perhaps could have filled a postcard. His pregame pep talk invariably contained the assertion: "Youse guys have two legs, two arms, and two heads, just like the udder guys." We never could decide if he was kidding or not. Nevertheless, we played our hearts out for him, sprinting until our guts burst, delivering bone-crunching tackles, kicking the ball high and far.

It was not until I got to college that I realized that we had not been playing soccer at all. Sure, occasionally we accidentally completed a pass or two—and even got lucky and scored some goals. One year, we even muscled our way to the state championship. But once I found myself on the field with give-and-go, step-over, swerve-passing guys who understood the game, I knew I was outclassed. I felt let down by my high school coach—and my soccer college playing days ended ignominiously after fall of freshman year.

Years later, I picked up the sport again. My first child was beginning to play in the local recreation league and I had volunteered to coach. I was determined to make the experience educational as well as enjoyable for my players. The first thing I did was to join a group of coaches who played pickup games among themselves on weekends. They included guys from around the world: powerhouse soccer countries such as Italy, Germany, Brazil, and Mexico, as well as smaller soccer-loving nations like Costa Rica, Israel, and Morocco. It was a tremendous education. What I learned, I shared with my players.

Ten years later, I had the seemingly bright idea of sharing soccer knowledge on a broader scale. I'd start a youth soccer magazine for the millions of kids who played the sport every week in the United States. It would draw on the expertise of the top coaches and national team players. As a magazine editor by profession, publishing a magazine was not a mystery to me. And so with two great partners, Horst Weber and Tom Mindrum, I launched *Soccer Jr.* magazine in 1991.

With the hard work of our small staff, and a big boost from the excitement surrounding the U.S.-hosted World Cup in 1994, *Soccer Jr.* grew rapidly, eventually becoming the biggest paid-circulation soccer magazine in the United States. At one point we were reaching over 400,000 readers. Unfortunately, our universe of advertisers began to shrink in the late nineties. Unable to continue to fund the venture, we eventually sold the magazine to Scholastic, Inc., of Harry Potter fame in 2001. But Scholastic couldn't work any magic on our title and in 2003 *Soccer Jr.* ceased being published.

All was not lost. Aside from helping to educate a generation about the beautiful game, much of what I learned during *Soccer Jr.*'s ten-year run can be found in this book. I am deeply indebted to the many soccer coaches and players who have shared their knowledge with me, especially Hall-of-Famer Efrain "Chico" Chacurian and Bob "Coach" Dikranian.

Joe Provey
Bridgeport, Connecticut
November 3, 2005

INTRODUCTION

Coaching youth soccer can be a wonderful experience that will enable you to share knowledge and good times with your kids and the youth of your community. I still receive warm greetings from the young men and women I've coached during the past twenty years. It's wonderful to see how the uncoordinated or shy six-year-old you taught and encouraged as a player is now a high school or college graduate, heading into adulthood brimming with confidence and fitness. It's fun to hear about what each remembers. It's also great to see how your former players have matured both as players and people—and how some are still involved in the sport, playing and preparing to coach their own children. Many of their parents remain friends as well. Occasionally, we share the good memories of our years on the sidelines together, whether it be how an Ivy-league-bound daughter scored her first goal in the wrong net or how a "B" team of kids, rejected by other teams, managed to tie a cocky squad of state champions.

Unfortunately, memories of youth coaching are not always golden. They are often blemished by disputes, misunderstandings, broken-hearted kids, and poor on-field and sideline behavior by both players and adults. Even worse, we've all read about the tragic confrontations between coaches and enraged parents. Coaches who understand their role and accept the responsibilities that go with it can avoid most if not all of these problems. But it's not automatic. It does not follow that just because you are a good-natured, well-meaning person that you will be a good coach. Some of the nicest individuals I have ever met were mediocre coaches—and worse, several actually did harm to the very kids they were trying to help.

With so much riding on how well you, as a coach, do your job, it makes sense to educate yourself about how to do the job right. *The Confident Coach's Guide to Teaching Youth Soccer* is geared to coaching kids between the ages of five and twelve. While it does not pretend to have all the answers, it will give you a very good beginning.

First, it will challenge you to consider the broader issues involved with what you are doing: the philosophy of youth sports, the importance of promoting safety and health, the constructive involvement of parents, and the development of resources beyond what you can personally deliver. You will find out if you have what it takes—and if you don't, what you can do to better prepare yourself.

Second, it will serve as a teaching manual for the proper development of soccer skills. Every skill will be dissected so you can see exactly what's involved. Coaching tips are provided for each skill. Nor do we forget about goalkeepers—there is a complete section on teaching goalkeeping skills.

Most importantly, *The Confident Coach's Guide to Teaching Youth Soccer* will enable you to quickly plan fun, productive practice sessions. It provides dozens of fun teaching games, many of which are appropriate for a wide range of ages and abilities, that you can use at practice. Select from the games based on the needs of your team, whether it be to improve passing, tighten up the defense, or tune finishing skills.

Mastering skills without developing tactical understanding is like driving nails without any idea of what you're building. So Part IV of this book, "Putting It All Together," is devoted to tactics. It will cover the principals of playing offense and defense as a team, provide tactical tools for penetrating opponents' defenses and shutting down attackers, and give useful advice about positions and formations.

Finally, *The Confident Coach's Guide to Teaching Youth Soccer* includes resources for coaches who want to pursue their soccer education further. There is a comprehensive section on rules (a must-read for any coach who truly wants to be confident) as well as lists for where to find just about anything related to soccer, be it a CD on the history of the World Cup or where you can order a quality pair of cleats.

KEY TO DIAGRAM SYMBOLS

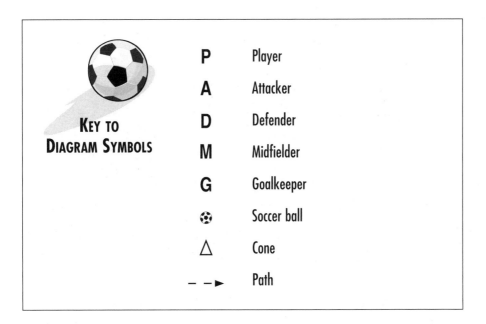

P		Player
A		Attacker
D		Defender
M		Midfielder
G		Goalkeeper
⚽		Soccer ball
△		Cone
– –►		Path

Part I
THE FUNDAMENTALS OF COACHING

CHAPTER 1

WHAT IT MEANS TO BE A YOUTH COACH

Forget everything you have seen on TV about being the coach of a team. Youth soccer does not need a kiddie version of Phil Jackson or Bill Parcells barking commands to his players and assistants. In fact, coach is a misnomer. What you really are, or will be, is a facilitator and teacher.

As a facilitator you will be the one who creates a safe, fun environment for practice sessions. You will also be the person charged with ensuring a good playing experience for every child on your team. You will—and should—seek help to accomplish these two things, but on most youth soccer teams it is the coach who has most of the managing responsibility. Try as I might, despite having capable "team moms" or "team dads" (managers), it was usually me at the end of the day with overall responsibility for the success of the enterprise.

The teaching part of the coaching equation is paramount. If you feel that you cannot teach the game, either because of lack of soccer knowledge or teaching aptitude, you probably should find a different way to help the team. Do not deprive your players of a chance to learn the game. It is not a lot of fun to play soccer without skills or understanding.

Even if you feel you can teach the game to a high level, commit to continue to improve. This might involve playing the game in your spare time, watching the professional soccer on TV or in person, attending coaching clinics, or taking a refereeing course to gain a firm understanding of the rules.

There will of course be a limit to what you can teach. You may have enough knowledge to handle a group of eight-year-olds but not thirteen-year-olds. If you find yourself in this situation, you have a couple of choices: hire a technical coach, often a skilled player from a local college, and work together on a curriculum. Or find a new head coach with the skills and knowledge your players deserve. As a former coach, you will be invaluable as a team manager or assistant coach.

Setting Your Goals

Youth soccer is not only about winning. In fact, a good youth coach is remembered by his players with respect, regardless of how many wins and losses there were. A poor one has the ability to turn a child away from soccer and sports in general for life.

Repeat the mantra: winning is not all-important until you actually believe it. It will help immensely if you make a list of the things that actually do matter. Think of this list as a report card and use it to grade yourself before and after every season.

Assessing Your Progress

Use the report card to help set goals for yourself. If you gave yourself a D in parental communication because parents were upset about having to play in a tournament on Mother's Day, make sure you include "better communication with parents" on your list of priorities. Score yourself low if a father complains that his child is playing far less than other children and make it a goal to develop a system so that doesn't happen again. If your report card says you have two or three players who seem lost on the field, resolve to get them more involved at practice.

**COACH'S
REPORT CARD**

*Grade yourself before and
after every season.*

Fairness to all players:

Do all players receive adequate
playing time?   A B C D F

Do you give players a chance to play
various positions?   A B C D F

Do you avoid putting too much pressure
on your best players?   A B C D F

Do you give equal attention to substitutes
and weaker players?   A B C D F

Team's performance:

Have team leaders emerged?   A B C D F

Do your players make offensive and
defensive tactical decisions on the field
without your direction?   A B C D F

Do your players exhibit support and care
for each other?   A B C D F

Regardless of your team's record, is your
team playing better at the end of the season
than it did in the beginning?   A B C D F

Individual performance:

Is every player on your team making
progress?   A B C D F

Have you assessed each player's skills
and discussed ways to improve areas of
weakness?   A B C D F

Is every player enjoying himself or herself? A B C D F

**COACH'S
REPORT CARD**

continued...

Practice sessions:

Do you have a plan ready to share with
your assistant when you arrive?   A B C D F

Is there a theme for each practice?   A B C D F

Do you avoid trying to teach too many
things at once?   A B C D F

Is everything you teach age-appropriate? A B C D F

Do you leave time for questions?   A B C D F

Is attendance good?   A B C D F

Game day:

Is your team mentally and physically
prepared?   A B C D F

Do you have your starting line-up, with
positions, before arriving at the field?   A B C D F

Do you know when and where you will
make your substitutions?   A B C D F

Do you allow enough time for warming up? A B C D F

Delegation of responsibility:

Have you found ways to get help from
parents in the running of your team?   A B C D F

Do you give clear instructions to your
team manager?   A B C D F

Communication skills:

Have you taken the time to explain your
goals for the team with parents, players,
and assistants?   A B C D F

Do you constructively answer parents' and
players' questions about playing time,
preferred positions, and other matters?   A B C D F

Do you make use of the Internet in your
efforts to streamline communication?   A B C D F

**COACH'S
REPORT CARD**

continued...

Attention to safety and health:

Did you ensure that players had adequate water and sunblock lotion on hand at practices and games?   A B C D F

Do you have a fully stocked first-aid kit?   A B C D F

Do you avoid smoking in front of your players?   A B C D F

Do you counsel kids on when and what to eat prior to games as well as for general fitness?   A B C D F

Do you counsel players on proper equipment, including shin guards, footwear, and keeper gloves?   A B C D F

Sideline behavior:

Do you model sportsmanlike behavior on the sideline?   A B C D F

Are you respectful of referee decisions, even when they go against you?   A B C D F

Do you use your time on the sidelines constructively by taking notes on players and overall team performance?   A B C D F

Do you avoid yelling directions to players during games?   A B C D F

CHAPTER 2

BUILD A PARENTAL SUPPORT TEAM

Coaching youth sports successfully involves creating two teams, one of kids and one of adults, usually parents. Here are the two key positions you will need to fill on your adult team.

The Assistant Coach

Begin by choosing an assistant coach. There will be occasions when you will be happy to have two adults on the sideline or at practices. An assistant can serve as a backup during medical emergencies or as a substitute when you cannot make a game or practice.

However, do not treat your assistant coach as a spare tire. Involve her in your practices and on game day. Give him specific duties, such as to watch the performance of the team and to make notes about what he see: goal-scoring sequences, defensive lapses, excellent series of passes, the number of corner kicks, shots on goal, shots off goal, good and bad clearances, and so on. Give her time to discuss her observations at half-time or after the game. Or, put him in charge of checking the field and bench area for safety, ensuring adequate water supplies and informing players about the upcoming schedule. Assistants can also encourage substitutes to stay focused on the game and help the coach keep track of playing time in order to avoid inequities.

Choose an assistant coach who shares your philosophy about coaching and with whom you communicate well. Your choice should complement your abilities. For example, if you are a male coaching females, choose a female assistant. If you have a long commute to work or must be away on business travel from time to time, choose someone who works close to home. If you have excellent soccer knowledge but not much experience with kids, choose someone who has worked with kids. Avoid selecting an assistant who feels it is necessary to call instructions to players during matches. Moreover, avoid having more than one assistant. Too many adults on the sideline add confusion and often tension.

The Team Manager

A good team manager, aside from the coach, is the most important adult on the team. Do not simply let the job fall to your spouse or your life may become consumed by soccer. Team managers (or their designees) are responsible for all off-field tasks, including organizing a preseason parent meeting, and making and distributing schedules, field assignments for practices and matches, and directions to away games and tournaments. They also do paperwork associated with registering players, collect registration and other fees, organize phone trees and fund-raising efforts, pay refs, buy equipment, attend club meetings, disseminate information about clinics, sign up for tournaments, get permission to travel out of state, and make the necessary travel arrangements.

If you find a good team manager, encourage her to delegate as many tasks to other parents as possible. Some jobs that are relatively easy to delegate include keeping the first-aid kit stocked, making sure corner flags are on hand for matches, checking to see if goals are secured to the ground, having water on hand at all times, assigning parents to bring oranges and juices for halftime, organizing postseason parties, and maintaining the team Web site (a good idea for any team that travels).

CHAPTER 3

PLANNING YOUR PRACTICES

It does not take long to plan a practice session—but practices will seem interminable to you if you do not. (See the recommended format suggested at the end of this section. There is also a practice-planning sheet you can photocopy.) Having your plan on paper will not only help you remember what you want to accomplish, but it'll also give you an easy way to inform your assistant coach about your plans. In addition it helps to keep you on schedule, so your practices do not end up running too long.

Several soccer educators recommend that you try to simulate the rhythm and pace of a match in your training sessions. For young kids plan practices so they last about fifty minutes. For older kids plan slightly longer practices, ranging from sixty to seventy-five minutes. Generally, your practices should not last longer than your matches.

For young kids focus the sessions around a basic skill (such as finishing) or a combination of skills (such as passing and receiving). For older kids you may choose to concentrate on a more advanced skill (e.g., side volleys or diving headers) or tactics (executing a wall pass or free kick, maintaining possession on throw-ins, or defending corner kicks). Concentrate on only one or two skills or tactical tools per session. Trying to do too much in one practice can cause the players to become distracted and to lose interest.

Following the demonstration segment of the practice, it is often helpful to break the team into two or more groups. This is when an assistant comes in handy. Be sure to rotate between groups so you can assess the progress of each player.

During practices coaches should try to keep kids moving. You can recognize an inexperienced coach or one who is not knowledgeable if you see lines of kids, five or six deep, awaiting their turn to perform a drill or exercise. This is not to say that you must have your players running about continuously. Brief rests of thirty to sixty seconds between activities are fine, with perhaps one longer break of three to five minutes halfway through the practice.

Besides keeping all the kids moving, you should keep your verbal instructions to a minimum. Try not to exceed three or four minutes of talk before getting to the action. Avoid long-winded explanations. There are more effective ways to make your points. When kids are practicing a demonstrated skill, for example, roam from pair to pair or group to group and offer individual critiques. During practice games that involve many players, such as keep-away, ask the participants to freeze when you blow your whistle. While they are frozen, quickly deliver your observation or ask for a child's opinion of the situation, and then blow the whistle again to resume play. A very effective way to communicate to kids, however, is to join in the game. It is amazing how much you can share—and show—kids while you are running around with them. Switch sides frequently, or play for whichever side has possession, in order to be able to share with all players equally.

Building a Practice Session

Your first job as a coach is to create practices where everyone has fun. Your second job is to teach skills and tactics. I have used the following format, recommended by many youth soccer educators, to do both.

1. Get kids engaged in a fun, warm-up game. (10 minutes)

Get kids involved as soon as they arrive to practice. Rather than allowing them to shoot on the goalkeeper until everyone arrives, get them started on warm-up games. For kids who have learned the basic passing and receiving skills, I usually have players form groups and play 5 versus 2 in a circle. Have five kids make a small circle about 7 or 8 yards in diameter. Put two kids in the center. The players on the outside of the circle pass to each other in any order. The ones in the circle try to intercept or deflect the passes. If a player in the center wins or deflects the ball, the player who has been in the center the longest joins the ring of players and sends the player who made the poor pass to the center. First pass is free (not contested). If there are not enough kids at first for 5 versus 2, they can begin with 3 versus 1 or 4 versus 2. As more kids show up, start a second group.

2. Demonstrate a strength-building exercise. (5 minutes)

Young kids do not really need to stretch before play. Despite what we have been told for decades, older kids probably do not either. According to the latest research findings on the subject, getting the blood flowing and raising the body's temperature is important, but stretching the various muscle groups is not. In fact, some researchers say that stretching may be detrimental to performance and increase the risks of injury. In addition to the warm-up game described earlier, jogging or dribbling around the field can be a good way to warm kids up. Once kids are warmed up, take this time to demonstrate one of the strength-building exercises (described on pp. 34 and 35).

3. Demonstrate one individual skill (or two related skills), a combination play, or a simple tactic. (5–10 minutes)

Most coaching manuals recommend focusing on one subject per session. Because soccer skills are closely interrelated, however, you may want to focus on one skill and review one learned at an earlier session. For example, while teaching chipping, you may want to review chest receptions. While working on corner kicks, you may also be able to practice volleys.

Many demonstrations involve more than one person, so it helps to have a knowledgeable assistant coach. You can, of course, select players to help with the demonstration as well. For very young players the demonstration may be showing how to make a push pass or inside-of-foot reception. For older kids it may be making wall passes or crossing from the flanks while dribbling under pressure.

4. Have kids practice what has been demonstrated. (5–10 minutes)

This part of the practice often requires areas or spots to be marked with cones. If possible, lay out your cones before practice so you do not have to stop and waste time. If this is not possible, enlist the aid of your assistant coach or players to set up the cones.

5. Have kids play a game designed to incorporate what has been demonstrated. (10 minutes)

There is a real art to devising and selecting the appropriate game for purposes of practicing skills and learning tactics. In addition to the many games described in this book, build a library of other games that work for you. You can see them demonstrated at clinics (often staged in connection with annual state meetings and at national coaches conventions). You can also find them in books, magazines, videos, CDs, and now on the Internet.

Do not become intimidated, however, by the number of practice games available to you. You do not need to know them all—a dozen favorites will do. Surprisingly, the same activity you use for seven-year-olds often works for seventeen-year-olds. Many skills do not really change as the players age—they simply happen at a much faster pace and over a bigger area. The beauty of this is that once you introduce a teaching game to your players, with a few modifications, you will be able to use it with the same group for many years.

6. Have kids play a small-sided game. (10–20 minutes)

This game can be a regular soccer scrimmage (e.g., two games of 4 v 4), or it can be a soccerlike game as long as it includes finishing. Many of today's national coaches lament that the U.S. youth soccer system produces lots of midfielders, defenders, and keepers—but not many strikers. They recommend that you incorporate finishing in this and other portions of your training sessions.

7. Cool down and make announcements to players and parents. (5–10 minutes)

Use this time to review with players what they have learned during the session. Encourage them to ask questions. Remind them about upcoming practices, matches, or other team events. Older players may use this time to lightly stretch muscles to prevent stiffness later.

Practice Planning Sheet

Warm-up game _____ ☐ minutes
Notes and diagrams:

Strength-building exercise _____ ☐ minutes
Notes:

Skill or tactic of the day/
secondary skill or tactic of the day _____ ☐ minutes
Notes and diagrams:

Practice Planning Sheet (cont)

Fluids and rest period (5 minutes)

Game that uses skill or tactic of the day _____ ☐ minutes
Notes and diagrams:

Small-sided (4 v 4) game or
small-sided scrimmage _____ ☐ minutes
Notes and diagrams:

Cooldown and recap   5–10 minutes
Notes:

CHAPTER 4

PROMOTING SAFETY AT PRACTICE AND ON GAME DAY

Even if you delegate safety checks to an assistant or to a parent, ultimately you are responsible for the safety of your players. Make copies of the "Safety Checklist for Coaches" that follows and hand them out to parents and players. Then tape a copy to a clipboard and consult it every time you take the field for practice or for a game.

Pay special attention to goals. Unlike cuts, blisters, and sprains, they can kill. I once saw a full-size goal be blown over on a gusty day. It came down with a heavy thud and missed a player by only a few feet. Goals must be securely anchored to the ground, either weighted by bags or stakes. Do not play or practice with unanchored goals. Many accidents with goals occur when they are being moved without adult supervision. Do not ask young kids to move a goal. It is too easy for them to cause a goal to fall upon themselves or a teammate. Finally, let your players know that you will not tolerate horseplay around a goal and that they are not to climb or swing upon the crossbar.

Sandbags, attached with secure straps, help prevent goals from tipping over on windy days.

Safety Checklist for Coaches

- [ ] Goals are anchored with anchor pegs or weighted bags to prevent tipping or blowing over. Unanchored goals can easily topple in high winds, while children climb upon them, or if children attempt to move them without adult supervision.

- [ ] Goals are made to today's standards. Homemade goals, often fabricated in local workshops, may have protruding bolts, net hooks, or anchor stakes that can cause severe injuries.

- [ ] Players are not wearing jewelry such as necklaces, wristwatches, bracelets, or earrings. Jewelry can become ensnared during play, causing injury.

- [ ] Warm-up area is clear of soccer bags and other items that could cause someone to trip. Many injuries happen before the match even begins. Keep warm-up areas clear.

- [ ] Benches, bleachers, and spectators are not too close to the sideline. The first 5 yards from the sideline should be kept clear to prevent mishaps and to allow players enough room to throw the ball back into play.

- [ ] There are water bottles for everyone—or a large jug and cups. It should be a parent's or coach's responsibility to have water at every match.

- [ ] Players are wearing sunscreen to prevent sunburn. Use team dues to purchase several containers of sunscreen and store it in the team's first-aid kit.

- [ ] The first-aid kit is complete and there is plenty of ice on hand. Your first-aid kit should include bandages, tape, gauze pads, cold packs, nonaspirin pain reliever, scissors, sting reliever, sunscreen, elastic wrap, and closure clips. Ice is invaluable for treating bumps and sprains, reducing swelling.

- [ ] There are no poison ivy, poison oak, poison sumac, stinging nettles, or other dangerous plants around field perimeter. Warn kids about what they may encounter while retrieving balls.

- [ ] The field is free of potentially harmful objects. These include damaged or inflexible corner flags that will not bend if fallen upon; stones, broken glass, and other debris on or near the playing field; drainage grates; and exposed sprinkler heads.

- [ ] Players are wearing adequate shin guards under long socks. Socks help keep shin guards in place, preventing trips.

CHAPTER 5

TEACHING THE RULES

Many coaches, especially novice coaches, do not take the time to teach players the rules of soccer in any great depth. They review the basics (i.e., what to do when the ball goes out of play at the end line or sideline) but steer clear of the offside rule and the differences between minor and major offenses. This may be fine for very young players, with whom only the most basic rules are enforced. It is not good for older players. To play with complete confidence, it is important for them to completely understand the rules. Knowing the rules inside and out will also make you a more confident coach as well.

The best way for you to learn the rules is to take a referee certification course. Many classes use videos to illustrate why refs make the calls they do. State and regional soccer associations offer the courses regularly across the country. Taking such a course is a good thing to do with your child as well—and may become a way for your child to earn money in the future. In the meanwhile review the basic rules described in this chapter. (For a full listing of the "Rules of Soccer," see Appendix A, page 143.)

○   A pregame coin toss determines which team will start with the ball. Play begins with a kickoff from the center circle on a field that is 110 to 120 yards long by 70 to 80 yards wide. All players start on their half of the field, and no one on the defensive team may enter the center circle until the ball has been touched.

○ Each team seeks to score by kicking the ball into the opponent's goal. A goal is scored only when the ball completely crosses the goal line between the goalposts. Two goals, one at each end of the field, measure 24 feet wide by 8 feet high. Directly in front of the goal is the goal area, 20 yards by 6 yards. Beyond the goal area is the 44-by-18-yard penalty area, which is marked to signify the only space where goalkeepers are free to use their hands. The penalty spot is marked inside the penalty area. At all four corners are flags and a small arc marked just inside the field. Teams play ninety-minute games, which are divided into two forty-five-minute halves.

○ Teams consist of eleven players, who can be deployed on the field in a variety of ways. The rule is modified for younger teams (see "Rule Variations for Youth Leagues").

○ The goalkeeper plays in front of the goal and is the only player permitted to put a hand or arm on the ball. All other players use their feet, thighs, head, and other body parts to control the ball.

○ Attacking players cannot get between the ball and the goal they are aiming for unless there are at least two defenders (one usually being the goalkeeper) between them and the goal line. If they do, they are offside. (For more on this, see "The Offside Rule," following.)

○ A free kick is taken to restart play after an infraction or a score, or if the ball has gone out of bounds over the goal line. There are two types of free kicks: A direct free kick can result in a goal without the ball having to be touched by another player on either team. An indirect free kick must first be touched by another player before a goal can be scored.

○ If the infraction occurs inside the penalty area, the nonoffending team receives a penalty kick. The ball is placed on a penalty spot 12 yards from the goal, and the defensive players must remain outside the area until the ball is kicked. The goalkeeper must remain on the goal line until the ball is kicked.

○ When the attacking team sends the ball completely over its opponent's goal line, the defending team takes a goal kick. The ball may be placed anywhere in the goal area and is not considered back in play until it has been kicked out of the penalty area.

○ When the defensive team sends the ball completely over its own goal line, the attacking team takes a corner kick. The ball is put back in play from the arc at the corner of the field. A goal may be scored directly from a corner kick.

○ If the ball goes completely over the touchline (sideline), the team that did not touch it last puts the ball into play with a throw-in. Throw-ins are taken from where the ball left the field and must be thrown with both hands while both feet are on the ground on or behind the touchline. A goal may not be scored directly off a throw-in. Throw-ins are the most frequent restarts; there could be more than fifty in a ninety-minute game.

○ Some games end in ties. Some go into sudden-death overtime, in which the first team to score (golden goal) wins. Some games that remain tied after overtime use a shootout to determine the winner. Each team takes five penalty kicks. The team scoring the most goals is the winner. If the game is still tied after five kicks per side, the shootout continues, with players from each team alternating shots until a winner is determined.

Offenses and Misconduct

Things become a bit more complicated when a player breaks the rules. There are three categories of offenses: major and minor offenses and misconduct.

○ **Major offenses** are those that involve physical contact or a hand ball. The victimized team is awarded a direct free kick from the point of the foul. "Direct" means that the kick can result in a goal without the ball having to be touched by another player on either team. This is a decided advantage over an indirect free kick (see later below). If a direct-kick foul occurs in the penalty area, the direct kick becomes a penalty kick. The ball is placed on a spot 12 yards from the center of the goal, and any player on the offensive team may shoot at the goal. The goalkeeper may move on the goal line before the kick. If the shot does not go in but stays in play, the kicker may touch the ball only after it has been touched by another player on either team.

○ **Minor offenses** do not involve physical contact. For these, including offside, an indirect free kick is taken from the point of the foul. Another player must first touch an indirect free kick before a goal can be scored. An indirect kick awarded in the penalty area is played like any other indirect kick.

Explain to your team that any direct kick foul that occurs in the penalty area will result in a penalty kick. All players must stand outside the penalty area, except for the kick taker and keeper, until the ball is kicked.

◐　Teams often defend against free kicks by setting up a "wall" to block the kick. A wall may consist of any number of players lined up shoulder to shoulder. The closer the free kick is taken to the goal, the more players in the wall; there are usually around five players in a wall. These players must stay at least 10 yards from the ball and may not move until the ball is kicked. A player from the offensive team is permitted to create an opening in the wall by standing in it and moving away when the ball is kicked, but the player may not push a defender out of place while doing so.

◐　**Misconduct,** which results in a yellow or red card, is called when offenses are serious enough to merit further punishment than a free kick. In cases of blatant or repeated fouls, the ref may issue a yellow card (a caution) to one or more players. Anyone receiving two yellow cards in one match is sent off the field; the ejected player's team plays shorthanded for the remainder of the game. For more serious fouls the referee can immediately issue a red card, ejecting a player from the game.

◐　A referee may warn a player to shape up before a yellow card is issued, but more serious acts (swearing, spitting at an opponent, and so on) will not be tolerated and will result in a player being sent off the field at once. Players will be cautioned and shown the yellow card if they commit any of the following offenses:

1. Using unsporting behavior: this includes pushing, deliberately handling the ball, faking an injury, and preventing the goalkeeper from releasing the ball.

2. Showing dissent by word or action: arguing with the referee, including (for a goalkeeper) leaving the penalty area to engage the ref in a debate.

3. Persistently infringing the Laws of the Game: this includes repeatedly committing fouls and failing to restart play properly after being warned.

4. Delaying the restart of play: this includes kicking or throwing the ball away to prevent a free-kick restart, throw-in, or corner kick, and excessively celebrating a goal.

5. Failing to respect the required distance on a free kick or corner kick: players must be at least 10 yards away.

6. Entering or reentering the field without the referee's permission.

7. Deliberately leaving the field without the referee's permission.

◎ Players will be shown the red card and sent off if they commit any of the following offenses:

1. Serious foul play.

2. Violent conduct.

3. Spitting at an opponent or any other person.

4. Denying an opponent a goal or an obvious goal-scoring opportunity by deliberately handling the ball.

5. Denying an obvious goal-scoring opportunity by an offense punishable by a free kick or a penalty kick.

6. Using offensive, insulting, or abusive language.

7. Receiving a second caution (yellow card) in the same match.

Commonly Misunderstood Calls

Lack of knowledge about the rules, more than anything else, can ruin the youth soccer experience. Save a lot of frustration by reviewing commonly misunderstood calls with your team—and ask the kids to explain them to their parents! Everyone involved in the sport of soccer needs a

MAJOR OFFENSES

1. Kicking or attempting to kick an opponent.

2. Tripping or attempting to trip an opponent: this includes using the legs or stooping in front of (or behind) an opponent.

3. Jumping at an opponent.

4. Charging from behind or in a violent or dangerous manner (unless the opponent is guilty of obstruction).

5. Striking or attempting to strike an opponent: this includes a goalkeeper's throwing the ball at an opponent.

6. Pushing an opponent.

7. Spitting at an opponent.

8. Holding an opponent with the hand or arm.

9. Deliberately touching the ball with any part of the hand or arm (except for the defending goalkeeper in the penalty area).

10. Making contact with the opponent before touching the ball when tackling.

(Note: The first six offenses result in a direct free kick if, in the referee's judgment, they were committed carelessly, recklessly, or with excessive force.)

good knowledge of the Laws of the Game. Here is a quick look at six of the game's often misunderstood calls.

Advantage

The referee retains the option of ignoring a foul if she believes the team that was fouled would lose an advantage—a quick counterattack or a good shot on goal. The ref may signal the advantage rule by extending both arms forward and shouting, "Play on!" This lets everyone know that she is aware of the foul but thinks that stopping play would benefit the team that committed the foul more than the team that was fouled. The advantage rule is usually applied in the attacking third of the field when the fouled team retains possession of

MINOR OFFENSES

1. Dangerous play—playing in a manner that could result in injury to the player or to any other player. Examples include attempting to kick the ball while the keeper is holding it or attempting to kick a ball close to the head of an opponent.

2. Impeding the progress of an opponent—blocking an opponent's path while not attempting to play the ball.

3. Preventing the goalkeeper from letting go of the ball.

4. Releasing the ball and then putting a hand on it again before another player has touched it.

5. Holding the ball for longer than six seconds after gaining possession.

6. Using the hands to control a ball that has been received from a deliberate kick by a teammate.

7. Using the hands to control a ball that has been directly received from a throw-in taken by a teammate.

8. Wasting time—using tactics to hold up the game.

(Note: The last five offenses must be committed by goalkeepers in their team's own penalty area.)

the ball or would lose a potential goal-scoring opportunity. The referee is ignoring the whistle for the good of the game. After a few seconds the ref can decide to stop play and award a free kick if an advantage does not materialize. Advantage is applied less often with young players, to whom referees are trying to teach what is fair and what is foul.

Charging

Charging can be fair or foul. When two players make body contact, the ref must quickly decide if they were both playing the ball. If a big guy and a little guy go after the ball, the smaller one may very well end up on the ground. But that is not necessarily a foul.

If a player looks at the opponent just prior to charging in, then it is very likely going to be a foul charge. When judging the charge, referees must read intent in the eyes and face and look for nonshoulder contact. A fair charge does not have to be weak. It can be hard, but it cannot be violent.

Hand Ball

No player other than a goalkeeper in the penalty area is allowed to touch the ball with any part of the arm, from the shoulders to the fingertips. But touching the ball with your hands is not necessarily a foul.

The referee must judge whether the hand ball was committed on purpose. A nondeliberate hand ball is not a foul. To fall and accidentally touch the ball is not a foul. A hand ball must be deliberate. A hand ball is deliberate when a player extends an arm to present a larger target or moves the hands toward the ball. Instinctive movements of the hands or arms to protect against being hit in the face, groin, or breast are not considered deliberate handling of the ball.

Female players are permitted to protect their chests with crossed arms. When they do this, they cannot move their hands and they have to keep their arms pressed close to their chest. They are not permitted to lift their arms or to redirect the ball with their arms or hands in any way. A ref who believes a player has moved her arms or hands may call a foul.

If a hand ball by a defensive player goes into the defended goal, the score counts because of the aforementioned advantage rule.

Obstruction

Obstruction is not allowing an opponent a clear shot at playing a ball while not in possession of the ball. Obstruction is fair when the ball is within playing distance (usually on the ground and about 3 feet away). Unfair obstruction is the often deliberate action of one player that impedes the progress of an opponent; for example, a player with or without the ball who backs into an opponent is guilty of obstruction. On the other hand, a defender who is caught off balance by a quick, clever move by an opponent may be unable to react. The ensuing collision is often wrongly called obstruction, whereas the correct call is unfair charging.

A player can legally obstruct if the ball is rolling out of bounds.

Slide Tackling or Tripping

A player slide tackles when he drops and slides on the ground in an attempt to win the ball or knock it away from an opponent. If, in the referee's judgment, the player is not attempting to play the ball, he may award a direct free kick to the opposing team. A careless or reckless slide tackle may result in a yellow card. If the ball is played first, however, no foul should be called—even if the slide tackle is followed by an unintentional trip.

Players often dive to create a foul. Diving is simply an act by a player to invoke the award of a free kick or a penalty kick by the referee. It is usually a desperate measure made by a player about to lose control of the ball. A player who sees a scoring opportunity slipping away is apt to be tempted to dive. Referees will often caution such players for unsporting behavior.

The Offside Rule

The offside rule is the least understood and most controversial of them all. Even the top professionals are at times unsure if they are offside or not.

Designed to prevent attacking players from hanging out by the opposing goal and waiting for easy chances to score, the law states that players are in an offside position if they are closer to their opponents goal line than the ball, unless they are in their own half of the field or are not closer to the goal than two opponents (including the goalkeeper) at the instant the ball is played. A player who is level (even) with the opponents is not in an offside position. To be called offside, the player must also interfere with play or with an opponent, or try to gain an advantage by being in an offside position.

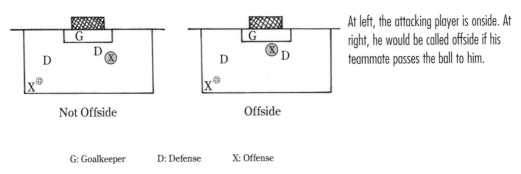

At left, the attacking player is onside. At right, he would be called offside if his teammate passes the ball to him.

Not Offside   Offside

G: Goalkeeper   D: Defense   X: Offense

A player's position when receiving the ball does not matter. What does matter is the player's position when the ball is actually played forward. A referee will not whistle an offside infraction until the ball is passed or shot. If, at the moment the ball is passed, there are fewer than two defenders (counting the goalkeeper) between an offensive player and the goal, the offensive player is offside—but being level with the last defender other than the goalkeeper is OK, and the player is not offside.

Spectators sometimes yell for an offside call when they see an opposing forward get a pass behind their team's defense. But if the player was onside when the ball was first played forward, there is no offside.

Making matters even more complicated is the fact that it is not an offense to be in an offside position if the player is not interfering with the play or gaining an advantage by being in there. A player who is in an offside position but who has no chance of reaching the ball before anyone else is not interfering with the play and should not be penalized for being offside. Offside should only be called if the offside player interferes with or distracts a defender or goalkeeper.

The referees must take a number of things into account when determining whether a player was interfering or gaining an advantage by being in an offside position. Was the player moving toward or away from the goal? How did the other players react to his presence? Had the player been hanging out near the goal and waiting for a "garbage" goal? Was the player injured? The answers to these questions help the referee make the correct call.

Making the correct call is especially tricky after a shot is made and it bounces off a post, crossbar, or keeper to another attacker. The original shooter might suddenly wind up in an offside position. If the second attacker shoots and scores at this moment, the goal might be negated with an offside call. It would depend on whether the referee felt that the first shooter's proximity to the keeper had affected the play.

Players cannot be in an offside position during a goal kick, a throw-in, or a corner kick.

Following an offside call, the opposing team restarts with an indirect free kick. It is taken from the spot where the foul occurred, unless the offside infringement is committed in the goal area. In this case the free kick is taken from any point within the goal area.

Encourage Respect for Referees

If the offside rule is still a bit confusing to you, just imagine how difficult it is for a referee, even with the help of an assistant referee, to call during a fast-moving game! Encourage your players to respect the referee's decisions, even when they seem unfair, and to focus on playing the game in a sportsmanlike way. Remind your players and parents that applying the rules to the myriad of situations that can occur in every game is not so easy. Much depends on the ref's interpretation of the rule and the ref's judgment as to the intention of the player. Did the player intentionally handle the ball with a hand or arm? Did the goalkeeper attempt to delay the game by taking longer than necessary to release the ball? Did a player attempt to gain an advantage by lifting a back foot off the ground before throwing the ball? Did the player in the offside position affect the play or not? As you can see, the ref's job is difficult. By understanding the fine points of the rules, you will be able to explain decisions to your players and avoid situations where, through ignorance, players feel the ref is "against" them.

Stress sportsmanship, especially for officials, at an early age.

Rule Variations for Youth Leagues

The game that has been discussed so far in this chapter is the standard outdoor game. For younger players, however, rules are often adjusted. Here are some of the common differences.

- ◐ **Equipment:** Not all players need high-tech cleats with replaceable studs or other fancy gadgets. In many organizations, including the USYSA, sneakers are OK for very young players.

- ◐ **Goals:** Most professional goalkeepers are six feet tall—or taller. Most kids are not. For that reason many youth organizations allow smaller goals. In AYSO, for instance, it is up to each particular region to determine what goal size to use.

- ◐ **Substitutions:** At high levels only a certain number of substitutions are allowed, and a player who has left a match cannot return. The FIFA standard is three subs per game. Youth leagues are often more flexible. Many have no limits on subs and allow for unlimited reentries.

◐ **Balls:** The pros use a size 5 ball, which is 27–28 inches in circumference and weighs 14–16 ounces. A size 5 ball may be too big for small children to handle; so many people recommend that children under the age of eight use a size 3 ball (23–24 inches, 8–10 ounces). Children eight to twelve should use a size 4 ball (25–26 inches, 11–13 ounces), and children thirteen and over should use a size 5 ball.

Use small-side games to provide more playing time and ball contact for younger players.

◐ **Game length:** The standard outdoor game is ninety minutes with a fifteen-minute halftime. Youth leagues play shorter games, often broken into halves (or even quarters) with a five- to ten-minute halftime. The following game lengths are good standards to go by: U-8, forty minutes; U-10, fifty minutes; U-12, sixty minutes; U-14, seventy minutes; U-16, eighty minutes; U-19, ninety minutes.

◐ **Fields:** Kids can fatigue quickly playing on a regulation field. USYSA recommends 20 x 30 (yards) for U-6, 30 x 50 for U-8, 50 x 70 for U-10, and 100 x 50 up to 120 x 80 for U-11 and up.

◐ **Small-sided:** Small-sided soccer (using fewer than eleven players per side) is the preferred way to bring youngsters into the sport. It allows for greater exposure to the ball (more touches) and increased skill development. AYSO strongly encourages small-sided games in younger divisions and permits such games for all divisions. In the USYSA, U-6 teams play 3 versus 3, U-8 teams play 4 versus 4, U-10 teams play 8 versus 8, and teams U-11 and older play 11 versus 11.

O **Miscellaneous:** The variations that can be made to the standard game are endless. Some leagues do not use keepers. Others do not apply the offside rule. Penalty kicks are not allowed in some leagues. Often, a score is not recorded. Any changes should be made with the interest of the players in mind. Fun is the top priority.

AYSO Recommendations for Different Age Groups Players

Age Group	Field Size	Per Team	Ball Size	Game Length (in mins.)	Misc.
U-6	25x20	3	3	32	no keepers
U-8	50x30	4	3	40	no keepers
U-10	70x50	8	4	50	keepers optional
U-12	100x50	11	4	60	with keepers
U-14	100x50	11	5	70	with keepers
U-16	100x50	11	5	80	with keepers
U-18	100x50	11	5	90	with keepers

CHAPTER 6

PROMOTING FITNESS AND HEALTH

It is sad, but many kids today are not fit enough to get the most from their youth sports experience. Soccer is especially demanding because it requires more running than most other sports, certainly more than the big three of American sports: baseball, football, and basketball. Obviously, you cannot correct a young lifetime of video games and TV in a single season, but you can make a start. The benefits to your players may very well last a lifetime.

Once your players are over ten years old, introduce one fitness exercise per practice session (before ten, kids will get all the exercise they need just by running around and playing). You can do it right after warm-ups. Explain the difference between reps and sets. Tell kids they can increase either as they begin to feel stronger—but not to overdo it or to exercise when they feel pain.

Encourage kids to try the exercises at home, especially during the off-season when they are not so active. Suggest that they stay in shape by working out a few times a week.

Discuss Good Nutrition and Insist on Fluids

Every family has different eating habits, and it is unlikely you are going to be able to change them a great deal. Nevertheless, explain to your players that they cannot play to their full potential without eating and

FITNESS EXERCISES FOR KIDS

Joe Luxbacher, a former professional soccer player who holds a doctorate in physical education management and administration, has devised the following exercises for kids.

Walk-ups

Have players stand near a bench or bleachers and step onto the raised surface, first with one foot and then with the other. Repeat. Beginners can try for three sets of five reps each, resting 30 seconds between sets.

Jump-overs

Have players stand beside their balls. On your signal ask them to jump over the ball from side to side. If they cannot clear the ball, have them stand a little behind it. Beginners can try for six sets of 45 seconds each, resting 90 seconds between sets.

Knees to chest

Have players jump upward, bring their knees toward their chests, and repeat as fast as they can. Beginners should aim for five sets of 15 seconds each, with a 90-second rest between sets.

Ball push-ups

Have players do push-ups while grasping a ball. Ask them to slowly lower their bodies until their chests touch the ball—and then to slowly raise their bodies to the starting position. Beginners can try for three sets of two reps each, with a rest of 30 seconds between sets. If ball push-ups prove too difficult, players can do regular push-ups instead. Remind them to keep their hands shoulder-width apart, back straight, and to raise and lower their bodies slowly.

drinking properly. Tell them to stock up on complex carbohydrates on the night before a game because they provide energy. Foods like pasta, bread, and rice will provide plenty of fuel. Fruits and vegetables are also a good source of complex carbohydrates. Ask them to avoid simple carbohydrates, which are high in sugar and do not provide long-term

**FITNESS EXERCISES
FOR KIDS**

continued...

Walking push-ups

This is a fun variation of the push-up. Have kids assume the regular push-up position with balls placed at their heads. Moving on with toe and hand "steps" see how far they can go. Two feet is great for beginners, 20 feet for older kids.

Abdominal curls

Have players lie flat on the ground with their knees flexed and arms folded on their chests. Ask them to rise slowly until their backs are at about forty-five degrees, and then to lower themselves slowly to the ground. Beginners should try for three sets of five reps each with about 30 to 60 seconds of rest between sets.

Sit-ups

Best done in pairs, have one player hold the feet of his partner to the ground. Tell the players to bend their knees slightly and to sit up and touch their toes. Beginners can try for three sets of fifteen reps before trading playing with their partners.

Running with ball

Ask players to dribble around the field, beginning slowly for the first lap and then at different speeds, including 20 yards of sprints. You may do this with a leader who decides when to sprint and when to jog or allow each player to go at his own pace and direction.

Pull-ups

Pull-ups with palms facing in or out are also good forms of exercise, but you are not likely to have a pull-up bar where you practice. Tell the kids to try them at home if they have a play structure or a chin-up bar in a doorway. When doing pull-ups with palms facing out, use a wide grip (hand shoulder-width apart); with palms facing in, use a narrow grip (hands six inches apart). Beginners can try for three sets of two to four reps each, resting a minute or so between sets.

Encourage all players to drink plenty of water throughout games and practice sessions.

energy. Explain that protein from meat and other foods is also good, but in limited amounts—and that they should avoid fats and sweets. Give some examples of healthy pregame dinners, breakfasts, and snacks that you know they can live with (see "Sample Pregame-Day Dinners").

Soccer tournaments can disrupt eating schedules, but players must have fuel.

SAMPLE PREGAME-DAY DINNERS

Pasta with grilled chicken, bread, a salad, fruit, and a glass of skim milk

Cheese and veggie pizza, salad, a glass of milk or milk shake

Chicken, mashed potatoes, coleslaw, rolls or bread, milk

Pasta with cheese and meat sauce, salad or veggies, garlic bread, a glass of milk or milk shake

The morning before the game, your players should go for complex carbohydrates and avoid fatty foods like sausage and home fries because they take longer to digest and can cause cramping (see "Sample Pregame Breakfasts"). Try to have breakfast at least one to two hours before the game. The closer it gets to playing time, the smaller your player's portions should be.

Advise kids to pack high-energy snacks that won't spoil. For snacks stay away from junk food and instead try celery sticks, pretzels, low-fat popcorn, oranges, or other high-carbohydrate, low-fat foods (see "Sample Game-Day Snacks"). Less than one hour before playing, your players should not have any food and should focus on being properly hydrated.

SAMPLE PREGAME BREAKFASTS

Pancakes with a little syrup (and no butter!), a glass of orange juice, a glass of skim or low-fat milk

Unsweetened cold cereal with skim milk and/or a bagel with jelly, a glass of juice, a glass of milk

Encourage your team to drink plenty of fluids before the game and as often as possible during the game. Remind children that they should drink even if they do not feel thirsty. Cool (not cold) water or sports drinks are the best choices for fluids during the game. Tell them to avoid drinks with sugar or caffeine because sugar slows the body's absorption of water and caffeine removes water from your system. Advise them to drink frequently in small amounts. Aim for three to six ounces every ten to fifteen minutes.

SAMPLE GAME-DAY SNACKS (GOOD FOR TOURNAMENTS)

Fig Newtons, Graham crackers, bagels, English muffins, hard pretzels, bread sticks, popcorn, cold cereal, rice or corn cakes, juice in cans or boxes, raw vegetables, dried fruit, granola bars, oatmeal-raisin cookies, blueberry muffins, dried banana chips, apricots, raisins, apples, and bananas

After the game is when players should fill up on meat and other protein-rich foods, which will help build and repair muscles. This is the time when they can indulge in that cheeseburger or pizza they have been craving. They can even have fruit juice, soda, or other sugared drinks in moderation—the sugar will help replace energy expended in play.

CHAPTER 7

COMMON INJURIES AND HOW TO HANDLE THEM

Compared with many other youth sports, soccer causes few serious injuries. As a result, it is common to see adults still playing the game well into their 40s, 50s, and 60s. There are, however, plenty of injuries in soccer. Here are some tips on how to handle them.

Sprains and Strains

Sprains and strains, especially to the legs and feet, are two of the most common soccer injuries. A *sprain* is a stretched or torn ligament. (Ligaments are the bands of connective tissue that join bones together. They help stabilize the joints.) Signs of a sprain are pain, bruising, and swelling. The player will usually feel a tear or pop in the joint. Severe sprains produce intense pain, as the ligament tears completely or separates from the bone. When this happens, the joint becomes nonfunctional. With moderate sprains there is some tearing of the ligament and instability in the joint. With mild sprains the ligaments are stretched but not torn and the joint remains stable.

A *strain* is a pulled or torn muscle or tendon. (Tendons are the cords of tissue that connect muscles to bone.) Typical symptoms include pain, muscle spasm, muscle weakness, swelling, and cramping. With severe strains the muscle or tendon is partially or completely torn, often incapacitating the player. With moderate strains the muscle or tendon is overstretched and slightly torn, and some muscle function is lost. With a mild strain the muscle or tendon is stretched slightly.

For all but the mildest sprain or strain, your player should see a doctor. Until you can get to the doctor, follow the "RICE" method:

- **Rest:** Immobilize the injured area and have your child sit quietly.
- **Ice:** Apply an ice pack (wrapped in a towel) to the injured area for ten to fifteen minutes.
- **Compression:** Wrap the injured area with elastic bandages.
- **Elevation:** Raise the injured area above the heart.

During the two or three days following the injury, continue to apply ice to the injured area several times a day, but only for ten to fifteen minutes at a time. Once the swelling and tenderness have subsided, you may want to try soaks in warm water or local heat application to reduce tightness or stiffness. Never apply heat while swelling is still present.

Head Injuries

Injuries to player's heads are less common than sprains and strains—but are the most worrisome for coaches and parents. Potential harm comes in two ways: repetitive striking of the ball with the head over a long period of time, and impact between the head and a body part of another player, the goalposts, or the ground.

Repetitive heading, according to many experts, is not something to be overly concerned about. Others disagree, especially for players who head the ball frequently in practice and games. Several studies suggest a connection between frequent heading and mild forms of brain damage, including diminished attention and diminished visual and verbal memory. The American Academy of Pediatrics has gone so far as to recommend against intentional heading until more is known about the risks. U.S. Soccer is managing a five-year study funded by a U.S. Soccer Foundation grant in 2001. It is expected to shed some light on the debate. The study has involved all players who participate on United States youth national teams (U-16, U-17, U-18, U-20, U-23 men; U-16, U-18, U-21 women). Each year, they are asked to fill out a questionnaire on their injury history over the previous year with a focus on head injuries. Each player must also complete a series of cognitive function tests. The study will attempt to find correlations between heading, head injuries, and changes in cognitive ability.

In the meanwhile most coaches continue to teach heading technique. None of the major youth soccer organizations have banned it, although the American Youth Soccer Organization (AYSO) tells coaches not to teach it to players under ten. All groups stress that teaching proper technique is crucial. Some are beginning to encourage players to avoid unnecessary heading. (See chapter 13 on teaching heading for a commonsense approach to teaching youth players.)

Unlike repetitive heading, there is no controversy about impact injuries that involve the head. They are potentially harmful. Of these concussions are the most dangerous. Every coach should know the symptoms associated with concussions and be extremely cautious should they suspect such an injury. This is especially true for young players whose skulls are not mature and are more susceptible to damage from concussions than are older players.

Concussions are not always easy to spot, so coaches need to be vigilant. If a player loses consciousness, then a concussion has definitely occurred. However, there may have been a concussion even if the player has not lost consciousness. Mental confusion and amnesia are common. Other symptoms include headache, fatigue, and dizziness.

DOES HEAD PROTECTION HELP OR HURT?

Many youth soccer organizations have approved the use of head protection but have not made it mandatory or recommended. While the various types of products, typically a padded headband or helmet, may reduce pain from minor knocks and discomfort when heading the ball, many neurologists are skeptical about their value. It is the movement of the brain inside the skull that causes concussions, they say. When a head is suddenly stopped, such as when it hits the ground during a fall, momentum carries the brain causing it to strike against the inside of the skull. This is what causes the damage. Protecting the outer surface of the head does little to cushion what's happening inside the skull. Some doctors speculate that adding weight to the head, even in the form of protection, may increase head mass and cause neck injuries. Furthermore, protective headgear may embolden kids to be more aggressive when heading the ball, leading to additional injuries.

Concussions typically occur when two or more players try to head the ball at the same time and collide head to head. Collisions with elbows, knees, the ground, or goalposts can also cause concussions. On rare occasions concussions may be caused by being unexpectedly hit in the head with a kicked ball.

Many concussions go unrecognized or are forgotten. This is dangerous because damage from concussions is cumulative. The more concussions a player suffers, the greater the risk of problems later. The worst-case scenario is successive concussions within a short period. Successive concussions can cause severe brain damage or even death.

CHAPTER 8

MAKING EQUIPMENT AND PLAYING CLOTHES RECOMMENDATIONS

As coach you will probably become a child's primary source of information about the equipment they will need to play soccer. In addition to league uniforms, ask each player to buy shin guards, soccer shoes, and a ball.

Advice about Shin Guards

For young players advise parents to focus on light weight, snug fit, and comfort. Remind them to place guards under socks, not over them where they can become entangled with another player's foot. It's not necessary to pay a lot for these guards when players are six or seven—low-end models that rely on wands or stiffeners sewn into the guard are fine—but it may be smart to spend a bit extra on the type with ankle padding if their child has a low pain threshold. They would not want one or two kicks to the ankle to discourage their budding soccer enthusiast.

As players get older, they need shin guards that deliver higher performance. That translates to less weight and more comfort and protection. Suggest shin guards with a hard molded shell that fits the leg snugly. Shin guards should extend from just below the knee to two or three inches above the ankle. Parents should expect to pay at least $15 to $20 per pair.

High-performance guards designed with attached (or detachable) ankle guards offer Achilles tendon and forefoot padding and often include cups or disks that protect the bones at either side of the ankle. Other high-performance shin guards, such as most OSI products that can be molded so they fit the contour of your child's shin, do not offer built-in ankle protection. Players who prefer these guards may decide to buy padded ankle guards that are sold separately or as part of a package.

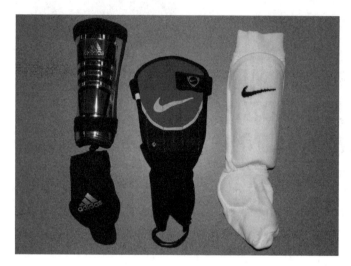

Ankle guards, shown with these shinguards, offer some additional protection from errant kicks.

For both younger and older players, it is important that shin guards stay in place. The old-fashioned way of securing shin guards—still preferred by some players—is the use of athletic tape. However, most shin guards come with straps and Velcro closures that do the job. Shin guards with attached ankle protectors stay in place better than others because they attach to the leg in two places—at the foot with a stirrup and at the calf with a top strap. For guards without ankle protectors, compression sleeves are the best way to hold the shin guard to the leg. Compression sleeves are elastic tubes that can be purchased separately and used with any guard.

Recommending Soccer Shoes

In soccer feet do most of the work. It follows that shoes are your players' most important piece of soccer equipment. They offer support and stability for running, protection for getting kicked or stepped on, and a stable surface with which to touch, receive, and kick the ball.

**TYPES OF
SOCCER SHOES**

There are four basic types of outsoles on soccer shoes, each designed for different playing surfaces or field conditions: turf, firm ground, soft ground, and flat. The easiest way to tell what playing condition a shoe is designed for is to count the studs. The more studs, the more evenly a player's weight is distributed and the better suited the shoe is for playing on hard ground.

If your team plays or practices on artificial surfaces or on fields with compacted soil because of lack of water or overuse of the field, suggest the purchase of a turf shoe. They are equipped with dozens of small rubber studs on the outsole that offer good traction and absorb shock that can cause stress to your feet. Turf shoes typically have more cushioning built into the heel than do soft ground shoes. Uppers can be synthetic or leather.

Firm ground outsoles typically have twelve medium-length studs or blades. They are as close as you can get to an all-purpose shoe and can be used on soft and hard ground. Many models have outsoles made of polyurethanes with two densities—hard at the tip for durability and soft at the sole and stud base to provide a little give and cause less stress on the foot. Some have outsoles made of rubber, which is even less stressful to the feet. Both Nike and Adidas make firm ground shoes specifically for women. The last (frame) upon which the shoe is built is narrow, which some female players prefer.

If players are fourteen years old or older and play often on soft ground, suggest a soft ground shoe with replaceable studs or with a bladed outsole designed for soft conditions. The studs and blades of soft ground shoes are longer, and there are typically only six to ten per shoe. Fewer studs or blades help prevent mud from clinging to the bottom of the shoes. Most players do not need replaceable-stud shoes until they reach high school age.

TYPES OF SOCCER SHOES

continued...

Flats or indoor shoes are similar to sneakers (no studs), but they may have soccer-shoe uppers. The outsoles are typically made of gum rubber and have more cushioning than found in shoes with studs. If you coach an indoor team in warm conditions where heat builds up in the shoes, the ability of the shoe to breathe or vent is important. Otherwise, players may end up with big blisters on the undersides of their feet. Leather or suede shoes have the edge over synthetic materials, such as microfibers, when it comes to breathability.

As it is with young players, the shoe fit is of paramount importance. If you see a player struggling with ill-fitting shoes, mention it to his parents. It is not fun to play with blisters from an oversize shoe that chafes — or to lose toenails because a shoe is too small.

Leather shoes are more forgiving than synthetics when it comes to fit because they will stretch slightly to accommodate the shape of the foot. Kangaroo leather stretches more than cowhide. Synthetic uppers, including microfibers, do not stretch. If the fit is not right to begin with, it is not going to get better as the shoe breaks in.

When discussing shoes with parents, suggest good but moderately priced shoes for each of the categories their child is likely to need. For the price of one pair of high-performance shoes, they can buy three pairs of shoes and be ready for every condition: indoor, turf, or hard ground and soft ground. If they can afford only one pair of outdoor shoes, recommend firm ground shoes.

For very young players tell parents to concentrate on fit. Over- or undersized shoes can be very uncomfortable and discouraging for a young player. Encourage parents to get together and swap shoes. Very young players rarely wear out a shoe before growing out of it. In addition to fit check to see that your players' laces are in good condition and firmly secured.

For older players explain that the type of shoe they wear will primarily depend on field conditions and playing surfaces. Advise them to have at least two pairs, one turf style shoe and one with studs or blades. The turf shoes, unless conditions are wet, are a good shoe to practice in as they cause much less stress to the foot.

Four styles of soccer shoes from left to right: indoor flats, firm-ground bladed cleats, firm-ground studded cleats and turf shoes

If your team plays in wet conditions often, suggest a shoe made with a synthetic or microfiber upper. Microfibers are lighter than leather when both are dry—and leather gets even heavier in wet conditions. Kangaroo leather, for example, can absorb more than 100 percent of its weight in water, whereas microfiber uppers absorb very little moisture and remain much lighter.

Buying a Soccer Ball

Be sure all of your players are using the appropriately sized ball (see chart following). It is much more difficult to learn skills if using a ball

WHAT SIZE BALL IS RIGHT FOR YOUR TEAM?

Use a size	for players aged
3	5 to 7
4	8 to 11
5	12 to adult

that is oversized. When asked for advice as to what ball to buy, recommend a hand-stitched, thirty-two-panel, polyurethane-covered ball with a latex rubber bladder to your players. They feel and bounce better than molded balls and are easier to control. Latex bladders do lose air relatively quickly, so recommend that your players buy pumps to keep their balls properly inflated. As coach invest in a good pump and keep it with your team equipment.

Use correct ball size for your player's age (see chart on page 47).

Prices of polyurethane balls range from under $10 to well over $100. The more expensive ones have several layers of covering to improve the ball's softness and touch, but these are unnecessary for most youth players. Tell parents to spend in the $20 to $40 range.

Practice Clothes and Uniforms

Advise players to come to practice in cotton shorts and T-shirts. In cold weather cotton sweatpants and sweatshirts are advisable. Requesting them to have a white and a solid color shirt, such as blue or red, will save you the hassle of bringing and regularly laundering training vests.

Buying uniforms is different from purchasing other pieces of equipment because the team or club typically specifies the style and maker. If you are asked for input, lobby for something that does not change from year to year and will stand up to repeated washings. Reversible shirts in two different colors are ideal.

Your gear bag should also include two goalkeeper jerseys in colors that contrast with the team's uniforms. Many jerseys incorporate forearm or elbow padding.

In cold weather tell your players to wear a cotton turtleneck under their uniforms. Advise both boys and girls to wear supportive underwear. Padded goalie pants and compression shorts make sense for goalkeepers.

Buying Keeper Gloves

Gloves help keepers make saves because they grip the ball better than bare hands and increase the area with which to stop the ball. They also protect the hands from the sting of the ball. Most kids will not need them until their opponents can strike hard shots—at ten or eleven years old—at which time youth coaches should keep several pairs on hand.

Once players begin to specialize in the goalkeeper position, suggest that they purchase their own gloves, one pair for matches and one for practice. As gloves begin to wear, the keeper can use the old pairs for practice and buy new ones for matches. Recommend gloves that are appropriate to your keeper's level of play. Expensive gloves have smooth palms made of thick, soft, spongy white latex foam. They provide more grip and shock absorption but will wear out faster than gloves with textured palms (that also cost less). For a recreation-level player, plan to spend $20 to $25 on a pair of gloves; for a travel player, $25 to $50. Pro-level models can cost well over $100. Advise players to purchase gloves one size bigger than needed. The extra half-inch fingertip length will help deflect shots that would otherwise end up in the net. The play (movement of the hand in the glove allowed by the extra size) also helps prevent the foam palms from tearing.

Other Equipment Coaches May Need

For a modest investment you can purchase a set of small goals. They fit in any car that can carry a pair of skis and are easy to set up. Portable goals have the advantage of making practice more like a game. When a child scores, the ball hits the back netting in a satisfactory manner. The best size for young players (four to seven years) is 4 by 6 feet. Cost is about $250 per unit. For older kids Kwik Goal, a manufacturer of goals and rebounders, recommends models that are 6.5 by 8.5 feet.

Cones work fine to mark goals as well. Cones are also helpful for marking boundaries, starting points, and running patterns. Disc (low profile) cones are the least expensive (about $1 each). Buy at least a dozen of them for marking boundaries. Taller cones (typically 15 inches) are easier to see from a distance, making them a better choice for goals. They cost about $5 each. Have at least six on hand.

Scrimmage vests will also make your practices go smoothly. There will be no confusion about who is on whose team. Prices range from $3 to $10, so you'll save some money if you can get your players into the habit of bringing their own T-shirts, one white and one of an agreed-on color.

Part II

THE ESSENTIAL SKILLS
AND GAMES THAT TEACH THEM

CHAPTER 9

TEACHING DRIBBLING

When teaching beginners, I introduce dribbling first because it is a solo activity that kids can feel good about learning. It involves pushing or tapping the ball with any part of either foot. For the very young player, it is the primary means of going forward to the opponent's goal. For more skilled players, dribbling is primarily used to elude defenders in the attacking half of the field while attempting to score a goal.

Confident Coaching Tips for Dribbling

1. Keep the eyes up as much as possible when dribbling. Use peripheral vision to keep track of where the ball is and what is happening on the field at the same time. It is OK for players to raise and lower their heads as they dribble. Just try to get them to avoid looking down all the time.

2. Keep the ball close to your feet so it isn't stolen.

3. Keep your body between the ball and the opponent (called shielding) to prevent opponents from tackling (stealing) the ball while dribbling. A would-be tackler must have a chance at the ball to attempt a steal. If an opponent pushes through the body of the dribbler, a foul should be called.

Step-by-Step for Dribbling

○ Use the inside (left) and outside (right) of your foot to move the ball forward with soft taps.

Have players use both feet when practicing dribbling so they're comfortable using their weaker foot.

○ The sole of your foot allows you to "offer" the ball to the defender—before withdrawing the offer and quickly moving off in a new direction.

○ Use your instep to move the ball forward or to make sharp cuts with the ball.

Dribbling Games to Use in Practice

Dribbling in a Square—After finishing your dribbling demonstration, get your players to try it. The best way to do this and many other drills is in a square or rectangular area, often called a grid. Mark the grid with cones or with paint formulated for making lines. You do not have to stick to a square. Circles work just fine for young kids. (For older kids squares are better because they simulate the straight lines and corners of a playing field.) In any case the confined area will allow you to see how they are performing without having to chase them all over the field.

As the children begin to move the ball, ask them to try different parts of the foot. In future practices ask them to move the ball with different parts of the foot *and* keep it close or pick up their eyes or change pace and direction.

Home Base—Mark off a square or circle in the middle of the field or use the center circle. Tell players that this area is the home base or safe area. Then have players line up outside the playing area with one ball for each of them. On your signal ask them to dribble to the "home base"—but not past it. This helps young kids develop ball control. For older kids reduce the size of the home base (e.g., use only half the center circle) and ask them to get there as quickly as possible. You can make this a race if you so choose (i.e., the last one in is a rotten egg), but avoid situations where the same players lose every time. (See the tactical version of this game, "Home Base with a Hornet," p. 141, for ideas on how to involve slower children.)

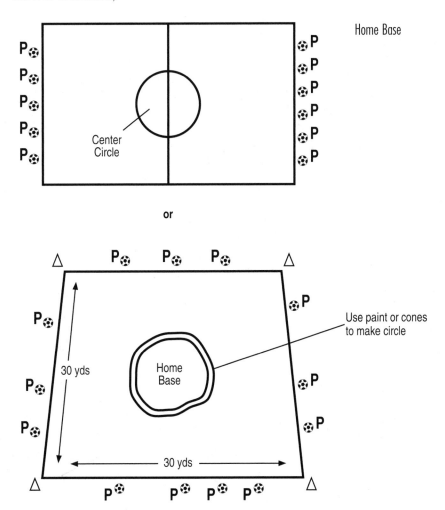

Home Base

or

Bomb Ball—Use cones to mark off a square area. Ten yards by 10 yards works well for a group of from eight to ten six-year-olds. Use your judgment for different numbers and ages. Ask the kids to dribble inside the area. Tell them you will occasionally toss a ball into the air so it will land in the area. Tell them to try to avoid being hit by the ball. This will encourage them to keep their eyes off the ground while dribbling.

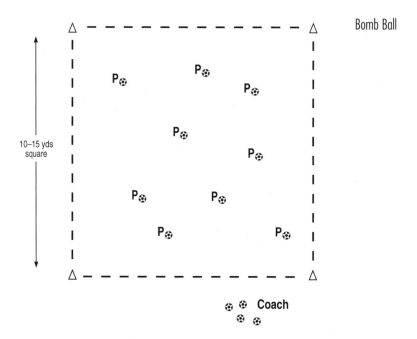

Bumper Car—Similar to bomb ball, but instead of tossing a ball into the area, ask the players to dribble and to try to avoid bumping into each other. This is another way to teach players to maintain good vision while dribbling.

Bumper Car Boot Ball—Again, this game is similar to above—with a twist: Ask the kids to dribble in the area and to try to poke or kick other players' balls out of the area as they dribble. This game promotes ball control. Players learn that there is less chance of having your ball booted out of the area if you keep it close to you. This is also a good time to introduce the concept of shielding.

Pac-Man (or Pac-Girl)—Perhaps the favorite of all dribbling games, begin by setting up an appropriately sized grid and ask players to dribble within it. Then select a Pac-Man or Pac-Girl to enter the area and try to tackle and boot balls away. The last player left is the champion. You may reward him or her with being the next Pac-Man.

Modify this or similar drills as necessary. Allow plenty of space in the beginning. Tighten the space to increase the pace as players improve. You can also vary the difficulty by adding more players. In Pac-Man, for example, have each player who has been "eaten" become an assistant Pac-Man.

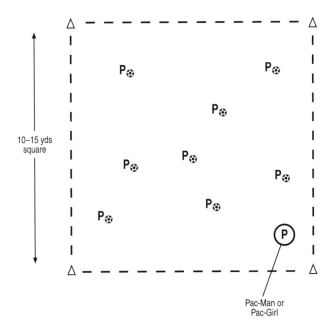

Pac-Man Game

10–15 yds square

Pac-Man or Pac-Girl

CHAPTER 10

TEACHING PASSING

Passing is another fundamental skill that requires years of practice in order to become proficient. The top players can drop long passes at the feet of a teammate. They can also swerve (curve) passes so defenders who are between the passer and the intended target do not intercept them. Youth players, however, are a long way from such feats. There are, however, several important types of passes you can teach. They include the push pass, the long pass or drive, and the chip pass.

The Push Pass

The push pass is the most basic and most useful of all passes. Use it to make either short distance or medium distance passes. A good push pass will be accurate (to the feet of a teammate or to the space where the teammate is running), well paced (not too slow or to fast), and smooth (not bouncing).

Players can make one- or two-touch push passes. In the former a moving ball is struck. In the latter the player stops the ball and then kicks it. The latter is, of course, easier. The former has the advantage of keeping opponents off balance and getting rid of the ball quickly before it can be stolen.

It is also helpful to teach kids to move to a new position every time they make a pass. The earlier they learn to become available for a pass immediately upon making a pass, the better they will perform on the field.

Confident Coaching Tips for the Push Pass

1. Place the heel of the nonkicking foot a few inches to one side of the ball (not in front or behind the ball!) and bring the toe down so it points in the direction you want the ball to travel. This is crucial. If the toe is pointing away from the target, the pass will go awry. This fundamental concept holds true for shooting the ball and making long passes as well.

2. For players having difficulty getting enough power into their push pass, remind them to lean slightly into the pass. It also helps to slightly bend the knee of the kicking leg and turn it outward.

3. If a player's push pass is bouncy and therefore hard for her teammates to control, it is probably because contact with the ball is too low (too close to the ground). Advise her to look for a spot on the center of the ball and to concentrate on striking it there, or slightly above it.

Step-by-Step for the Push Pass

O   Stride to the ball with energy. Push passes will be quite weak if a player tries making them from a standstill.

O   Place the nonkicking foot a few inches to the side of the ball (more for older players) and bend the knee slightly for balance.

Emphasize correct positioning of the non-kicking foot; it will carry over into many other skills.

○ Turn the kicking foot perpendicular to the direction of the pass, with toes higher than heel, and lock your ankle.

○ With the inside of the foot, make contact with the center of the ball. Swing the kicking leg forward from the hip and knee.

○ Follow through with the kick in the direction you want the ball to go. The foot should remain pointed outward and the ankle, locked. You may lean slightly back as you follow through.

The Long Pass

The long pass, or drive, requires strength, so it is not something to teach until your players are ready for it. The same kick, with slight modifications, can be used for goal kicks, corner kicks, long-distance shots, and free kicks. A successful long pass requires accuracy (both in direction and distance) and height (enough to put it over the heads of defenders).

Confident Coaching Tips for the Long Pass

1. As with the push pass, point the nonkicking foot in the direction you want the ball to go. Instead of planting this foot alongside the ball, however, place it a few inches behind the ball.

2. To achieve any distance, the ankle must be locked (held rigid) with the toes held slightly lower than the heel (about thirty degrees). Locking the ankle is a common omission on the part of young players. A floppy ankle absorbs most of the power of their kicks.

3. The lower you strike the ball, the higher it will go. For a kick of medium height, strike the ball a couple of inches below the center. For maximum height, such as when taking a goal kick, strike the ball just above the turf. Your toe should actually go under the ball. Take care, however, not to catch it in the turf!

4. Achieve greater distance by lengthening your approach to the ball (when possible) and by lengthening the backswing of your leg.

5. When kicking goal kicks, approach the ball from a slight angle to the direction you want the ball to go. Shorten your steps as they get close to the ball so you can place your nonkicking foot beside and slightly behind the ball.

Step-by-Step for the Long Pass

- ⟡   Approach the ball at a slight angle and shorten your steps as you get close to the ball.

- ⟡   Plant your nonkicking foot beside and slightly behind the ball.

- ⟡   Lean back slightly and swing your leg backwards from the knee and hip.

Demonstate how to lock the ankle for kicking. It's key for striking the ball well.

Approaching the ball from an angle allows players to generate kicking power with their body as well as their leg.

- ⟡   With ankle locked, strike under the ball with the instep of your foot.

- ⟡   Allow your follow through to carry you past the original position of the ball.

Chipping

The chip is typically used as a surprise pass. Use it to lob the ball over defenders' heads to an onrushing teammate. Or, use it to score goals when a goalkeeper ventures too far out of the net, such as on a breakaway. The key to a chipped ball is to strike it accurately and very low—there no need for power here.

Confident Coaching Tips for Chipping

1. The farther you bring your foot back and the longer your follow-through, the farther your chip will travel.

2. Use a short stroke for short-distance chips.

3. For accuracy keep your head down, looking at the spot on the ball you want to hit.

4. For better control when chipping, balance on your nonkicking foot by bending your knee.

5. To get more height on your chip, keep your heel low to the ground and make contact under the ball. For a lower, longer chip, hit the ball a little higher.

Step-by-Step for Chipping

○ Approach the ball from a slight angle.

○ Plant your nonkicking foot alongside and slightly behind the ball.

○ Swing your kicking foot (ankle locked) back behind your body from hip and knee.

○ With your heel close to the ground, drive your toe under the ball, striking it with your instep.

○ Make a short follow-through in the direction you want the ball to travel.

Chipping is tough to master. Tell players to stab the space between turf and ball to do it properly.

Passing Games to Use in Practice

Passing Catch (for all types of passing) — Not really a game, but a great exercise for players of all ages: simply have your players pair up and begin to "play catch." Instead of gloves, of course, they will be using their feet. Ask them to concentrate on making accurate passes that are not too strong or too weak (be they push passes, long passes, or chips) to their partners.

Once players achieve some proficiency, ask them to move to a new position several yards away after making every pass. Young players may use two touches (or as many as they need) to stop and prepare the ball for each pass. As players become more accomplished, they may try one-touch push passes. Want to add some excitement? Ask players to count the number of passes they can complete before a miss (a pass that does not reach or goes past the receiving partner).

Under the Bridge (for push passes) — Young kids love this game. Divide players into groups of three. Ask one player to stand between the other two and to spread his legs wide. The two remaining players take turns making push passes to each other, through the legs of their partner. When one player makes five successful passes, he moves to the center and the game continues. Vary distances depending on the age and skill level of the players.

Shooting Hoops (for chipped passes) — Place a hoop or paint a circle on the ground. Have players take turns trying to chip balls in the hoop or circle from about 10 to 20 yards away (depending on age). You can award points for "baskets" if you want to. As players improve, try

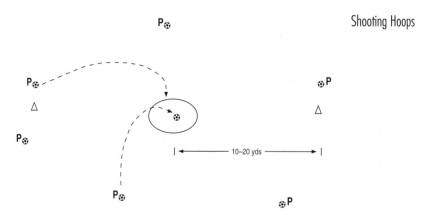

Shooting Hoops

lengthening the distance to the hoop. You can also make this game more challenging by using a clean plastic trash barrel instead of the hoop as the basket, rolling the balls to players so they can practice chipping a moving ball, or by erecting a net between the players and target.

Soccer Monkeys (for push passes and chips) — Divide players into groups of three players. Choose one player as the monkey. Ask the other players to stay 10 to 15 yards away from the monkey and to try to complete passes to each other without him stealing the ball. When the monkey wins the ball, the player who made the last pass becomes the new monkey and the original monkey takes his place.

There are many ways to vary this fundamental game (often used as a warm-up for high-level players). If young players are having difficulty stealing the ball, change the rules so they only have to deflect a pass. You can involve more players by adding one or two more passers and another monkey.

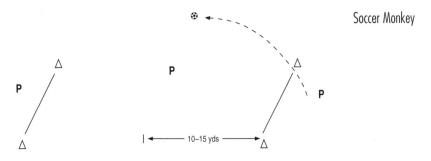

Soccer Monkey

Soccer Golf (for all types of passes) — When the weather is very hot, this low-exertion game may be just the thing. Place cones at varying intervals of from 30 to 60 yards. Divide players into pairs or trios and tell them they must pass their balls so they touch each cone in the sequence you devise. You can even assign "pars" for each "hole."

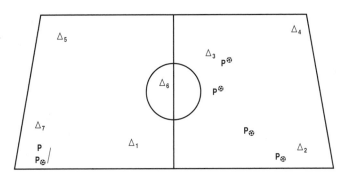

Use games, such as Soccer Golf, to improve accuracy of all types of passes.

CHAPTER 11

TEACHING
RECEIVING

Receiving a passed ball is a lot more than simply stopping balls that come your way. It involves several concepts: anticipation of where you will play the ball, controlling the ball, eluding a nearby defender, and preparing the ball for your next play. Receiving the ball can be done with any part of the body except the arms and hands. It is usually done with the feet (instep, sole, inside, or outside). It can also be done with the chest or inside of the knee or thigh.

Receiving Rolling Balls

With very young players it is enough to get them to learn how to meet the ball with the inside of either foot and to control it. As players mature teach them how to prepare the ball for passing or shooting, that is, so it goes a few feet in the direction they want to play the ball next—usually toward their opponent's goal. For more advanced players teach them how to receive and pivot away from a nearby defender in one fluid motion.

Confident Coaching Tips for Receiving Rolling Balls

1. Spread your legs apart as you prepare to receive the ball.
2. Look around prior to receiving the ball. Decide what you are going to do with the ball before you receive it whenever possible.

This habit will help you react more quickly to oncoming defenders and passing opportunities.

3. Use the arch of the foot to "catch" the ball.

4. Practice receiving the ball with both feet so you can handle more game situations.

Step-by-Step for Receiving a Rolling Ball

◎   Face the teammate from whom you expect a pass. This lets her know you are ready!

◎   Move quickly to meet the ball when it is passed to you.

Once players master receiving the ball, teach them to use that first touch to prepare the ball for a pass or shot, or to evade a defender.

◎   Meet the ball with the inside of either foot. It helps to raise the toes to prevent the ball from skipping by. Bend the knee of the nonreceiving leg for balance. Allow your foot to become soft upon contact to prevent the ball from bouncing too far away.

◎   In low pressure situations allow the ball to bounce a few feet toward the opponent's goal.

◎   In medium-pressure situations give way slightly with your foot and "pull" or guide the ball to the side and pivot.

◎   Dribble or play the ball to a teammate.

Receiving Balls in the Air

Very young players do not need to learn this skill for the simple reason that the ball rarely gets in the air. But once your players are able to make longer, higher kicks, being able to receive balls in the air becomes invaluable. Instead of wasting time chasing bouncing balls, your players will be able to control the ball before an opponent gets there and have more time for passing or shooting.

Confident Coaching Tips for Receiving Balls in the Air

1. Encourage players to glance around the field before they receive the ball. If a defender is moving toward them, they will be able to play the ball in the opposite direction.

2. Hold the receiving foot about one foot off the ground and level.

3. Use a soft touch so the ball rolls off the receiving foot, not bounces off it.

4. Juggling is a good way for players to prepare for learning this skill. Encourage them to learn how. Once good at it, they can practice receiving high balls while juggling by hitting every fifth or sixth juggle high in the air and then receiving it.

Step-by-Step for Receiving Balls in the Air

◐ Move into position so you can receive the ball in front of your body.

◐ Allow your weight to rest on the nonreceiving leg; bend this leg slightly at the knee for balance and to help cushion the reception.

Players should keep their ankle firm but not stiff when receiving a ball in the air.

◐ Raise the receiving foot about one foot off the ground, in line with the falling ball. Hold the foot level with the ground.

◐ On contact with the ball, "give" with your foot and leg and gently lower your foot to the ground.

Once players can drop the ball to the ground with control, have them try touching the ball to prepare it for their next play.

◐ Dribble or prepare to pass by pushing the ball forward to your right or left.

Receiving Balls on the Chest

The chest is a handy way to control a passed ball when it arrives too high to stop with your feet—or when using your foot might mean a high-foot call by the referee. Mastering the chest reception will also add speed to your players' game, allowing them to shoot or pass without even allowing the ball to hit the ground. (See dangerous play in glossary.)

Confident Coaching Tips for Chest Receptions

1. Girls with developing or developed breasts should make contact with the ball higher on the chest than boys—between the chin and the breasts. Encourage the use of sports bras for comfort and protection while playing.

2. Let the ball hit the chest muscle, not the sternum (center chest bone), to prevent the ball from bouncing too far away.

Step-by-Step for Chest Receptions

◐ Get your body into position to receive the oncoming ball with your chest.

○ Bend the knees and arch your back to create a flat surface upon which to meet the ball.

When players have mastered the chest reception, demonstate how the chest can be use to redirect the ball.

○ Give slightly on contact to cushion the ball.

○ As the ball hits the ground, take or prepare the ball in the direction you plan to go.

Receiving Games to Use in Practice

Hub of the Wheel (for receiving rolling balls or balls in the air)—Have six or seven players form a 20-yard to 30-yard circle and ask one player to step inside it. Distribute balls to half the players around the circle. Players with balls pass or toss them to the center player in turn. The center player must receive (with feet or chest) each pass and pass it to a player who does not have a ball. When using this game for receiving rolling balls, ask the center player to make simple one-touch or two-touch push passes or you can have her pivot prior to passing the ball. Once each player around the circle has made two or three passes, change the center player.

Chest Challenge (for receiving balls with the chest)—Mark circles with paint or cones. Have one player stand inside the circle and a partner stand 10 to 15 yards away with a ball. Ask the player with the ball to toss it in the air so it lands in the circle. The player in the circle must

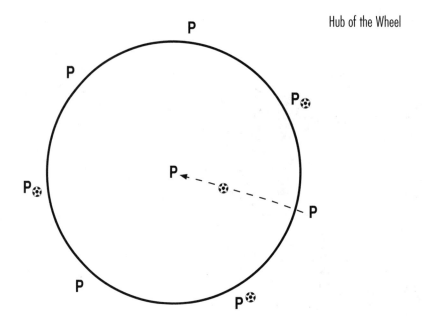

Hub of the Wheel

receive the ball with his chest and prevent it from rolling outside the circle. If it does, the player on the outside may take a turn inside the circle. Use 5-yard-diameter circles to start. Reduce the diameter of the circles as the ability of your players to control the ball improves. Use this game for receiving other types of passes as well.

Chest Challenge

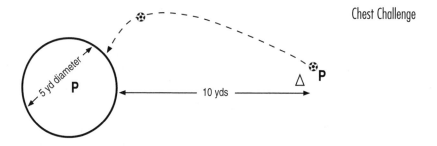

CHAPTER 12

TEACHING
HOW TO SHOOT

According to many national level coaches, shooting is not taught enough to players. Therefore, the United States produces very few high-level goal scorers. That is not really your first concern. The enjoyment of your players is. Fortunately, there is no conflict here because of all the skills, the player favorite is shooting. Any type of shot that puts the ball in the goal is OK. You will find your players using everything from the push pass to pokes with toes, knees, and heels, but there are several classic shots that you should teach them. They include the instep power drive, the half volley, the side volley, and the full volley.

Teaching the Instep Power Drive

This skill builds on much of what was learned with passing. The approach and placement of the nonkicking foot is very similar to that of the push pass (which can also be used for shooting, especially from close range).

Confident Coaching Tips for Instep Power Drive

1. An angled approach to this or any other type of kick increases power. The angle allows you to get more of your body into the kick because it automatically causes it to rotate as you hit the ball.

2. When running to the ball, use small, quick steps. Doing so will make it easier to time your last step so you can plant your non-kicking foot beside the ball.

3. The key to keeping your shots from skying over the crossbar is to keep your foot motion parallel to the ground. It helps to lean slightly over the ball as you make your kick and to keep your toe pointing down during your follow-through until you are about to land.

4. It is important to get shots off quickly—but not to rush them. Teach players to gain valuable time by making a move to throw a defender off balance before shooting.

Step-by-Step for Instep Power Drive

◐ When possible, approach the ball from a slight angle.

◐ Plant your nonkicking foot 10 to 12 inches beside the ball (aimed at your target) and draw your kicking leg back well behind your body.

The power drive is not intuitive for most players. Sometimes it helps to move the player's body into the correct position.

Explain that having the body over the ball upon shooting it will help keep the shot low and difficult for a keeper to save.

○ Swing your kicking leg forward from the hip and knee, keeping your body and head over the ball.

○ With your instep perpendicular to the ground (toe pointing down), make contact with the ball on the instep (the middle part of your shoe's tongue and laces).

○ Follow through forward in the direction of your kick, not upward.

Teaching the Half Volley

A half volley, also known as shooting the ball on the short hop, is a good way to surprise defenders and goalkeepers. Instead of controlling a bouncing ball, the player strikes it. The key to success is timing—you have to hit the ball just after it bounces. It is a skill more suited to players with several years of experience.

Confident Coaching Tips for the Half Volley

1. Half volleys happen at high speed, so there is no time to draw your leg all the way back. Take a short backswing instead.

2. Swing your kicking leg forward from both the hip and knee.

3. Keep the ball from sailing over the crossbar by keeping the toes of your kicking foot pointing down and moving parallel to the ground throughout the kick.

Stress a low follow-through with the kicking foot when teaching the half volley.

Step-by-Step for the Half Volley Shot

O   Approach a bouncing ball quickly, timing your run so you end up very close to where the ball will bounce.

O   Try to place your nonkicking foot beside the ball as you take a short backswing with your kicking foot.

O   Strike the ball with your instep just after it hits the ground and starts to rise.

O   Make a short follow-through in the direction of your kick, not upward, and land on your kicking foot.

Teaching the Side Volley

The side volley, like the half volley and full volley, allows you to take unexpected shots. Use it for high bouncing balls near the goal. It takes time and patience to perfect, but the spectacular goals that result from knowing how to do it make it worthwhile.

Confident Coaching Tips for the Side Volley

1.   When getting ready to make a side volley, bend your nonkicking leg slightly and lean away from where you expect to make contact with the ball.

2.   If you are kicking with your right foot, lower your left arm toward the ground as you lean and raise your right arm to help lift your right side. Do the opposite if you are kicking with your right foot.

3.   Remember to hit the ball in the middle to drive it parallel to the ground or hit it slightly downward. Extend your kicking leg fully on the kick.

4.   Depending on the height at which you strike the ball, you may be able to remain standing.

Step-by-Step for the Side Volley

O   Move into position so the ball will land in front of you.

O   Point your nonkicking foot at your target and balance your weight on it.

O   Lean away from the path of the ball and swing your kicking leg up. Bend your kicking leg back as you do so.

○ Allow your body to fall away and strike the ball in the middle with your instep. Swing mainly from the knee and try to time your kick so you hit the ball when it reaches waist height.

○ Follow through so your body lands slightly past where you made contact with the ball.

Enlist help from assistants when teaching difficult skills, such as the side volley.

Teaching the Full Volley

As players get older, defenders get better. Therefore, there are fewer shooting opportunities during a match. By adding the full volley to the skills repertoire of your players, they will be able to make the most of more of their chances when a ball bounces toward them. Full volleys are struck almost exactly as you strike a rolling ball with two exceptions: the kicking leg and foot must be raised slightly to hit the ball squarely with your instep, and the follow-through should be short to prevent the shot from rising.

Confident Coaching Tips for the Full Volley

1. You know you're volleying well if their shots have a top (forward) spin. (Topspin makes shots very tough for keepers to handle.)

2. Your knee, body, and head should be over the ball when the ball is struck.

3. Your foot should be perpendicular to the ground, with ankle locked, when the ball is struck.

Step-by-Step for Taking the Full Volley

○ Approach a bouncing ball straight on or from a slight angle.

○ Plant the nonkicking foot 10 to 12 inches beside the ball, pointed in the direction of the shot.

○ Bring the kicking foot back behind your body and extend it, so it is in-line with your leg.

○ Lock your ankle and kick forward with your hip and knee, keeping your toes pointed down. Make contact with the middle of the ball when it is about a foot off the ground. Land on the kicking foot well beyond your initial contact with the ball.

Teaching How to Take a Penalty Kick

Penalty kicks (PKs) are fun to take if you know what you are doing—and nerve-racking if you do not. Give your players an edge by devoting at least one practice session every year to taking them. Instruct younger players to focus on selecting a target to either side of the keeper and driving the ball there with the inside of their foot (as with a push pass) or their instep (as with a power drive). Once they are a bit older (when keepers can read a kicker's approach), you may want to introduce deceptive penalty kicks.

Confident Coaching Tips for Penalty Kicks

1. Choose a target and envision the mechanics of your shot before stepping to the ball and taking it.

2. Explain to your players that this deceptive PK is an exception to the basic rule of shooting. You do not point your nonkicking foot at the target. This will fool many keepers and cause them to lean in the wrong direction.

3. It will be easier to kick the ball accurately if you lean slightly left when taking this shot right-footed; lean right when taking the shot left-footed.

Step-by-Step for Taking the Penalty Kick

○ Approach the ball from a slight angle or straight on from about 8 feet away.

○ Place your nonkicking foot 10 to 12 inches to the side of the ball, aimed away from your target spot.

○ Swing your kicking foot from your hip and knee, toe pointed down and ankle locked.

○ Near the end of your kick, point your kicking foot outward, strike the ball with the inside arch of your foot at your target.

○ Make a short follow-through in the direction of your shot.

Tell players to disguise their intention to use the arch to shoot until the last instant.

Shooting Games to Use in Practice

New Use for Old T-Ball Tees (for side volleys)—Adjust the tees to their lowest height and place a soccer ball on top of it. Ask players to pair up. One player side volleys the ball to his partner several times and then the pair switches places. Gradually have players increase the height of the tee until they feel confident about striking a ball placed at waist height.

Toss and Volley (for half, side, and full volleys)—Ask players to toss the ball into air so it will land a few yards ahead of them (or to the side for side volleys). Instruct them to move quickly to the ball and shoot after the first bounce. Obviously, this game is best done against a wall or net—or in pairs, with players taking turns as shooter. Begin at a distance of about 10 yards. Make targets so players can practice their accuracy. Increase distance as they become more successful. Once they've mastered volleying bouncing balls, try striking them before the ball hits the ground.

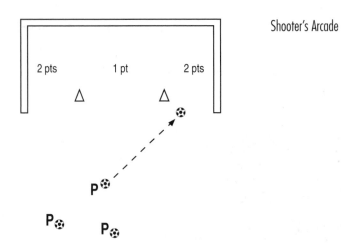

Shooter's Arcade

Shooter's Arcade (for all types of shots)—Turn the simplest of shooting drills into a fun game that will improve your player's shooting accuracy. Simply divide the goal into thirds using cones. Give out two points for scoring to either side and one for scoring in the middle. Change the scoring system as you see fit.

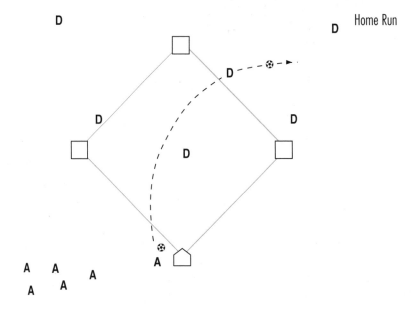

Home Run

Home Run—Adapted from baseball, this is a fun shooting and passing game. Position home plate in front of a goal and mark the bases as you would with baseball. Divide players into two teams and ask one team to assume positions in the field. The "pitcher" may either push pass or bowl throw the ball to the "batter," who "hits" by kicking it as far as possible. The batter tries to round the bases before the opposing team can shoot the ball into the goal. Field players may pass the ball in order to set up the best possible shot. You may play with outs (when the batter does not reach home plate before a goal is scored, it is an out) or allow everyone to have one at bat per inning. One goal counts as a "run."

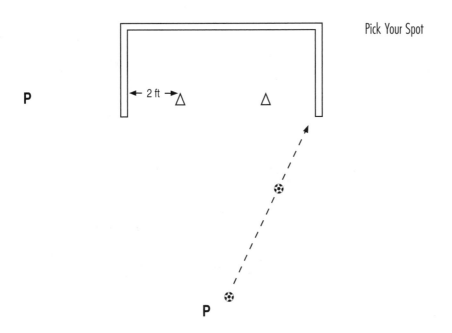

Pick Your Spot

Pick Your Spot (for PKs)—Divide your team into groups, the smaller the better. Using goals and cones or cones only, set 2-foot wide minigoals at each post. Line the players up, each with a ball, 12 yards away from the goal. Ask them to call out right or left and to execute a PK or deceptive PK accordingly. After each player has been able to take ten or fifteen shots, get rid of the minigoals and give your keepers an opportunity to practice stopping PKs. Use a single or double elimination to see who are your best PK takers.

CHAPTER 13

TEACHING
HOW TO HEAD

For kids under nine years old, teach proper technique with lightweight balls such as Nerf soccer balls, size 3 balls, or even balloons. This allows the child to perfect technique without anxiety about getting hit in the face with the ball. Introduce heading with age-appropriate balls when kids need this skill to play—not usually before ten years old. Before that there are few chances to head the ball because, aside from punts, few balls are driven into the air. In your training sessions focus on proper technique.

Advise players not to head the ball if it can be better played with their chests or feet. Explain that it makes no sense to use headers to pound the ball aimlessly up field.

Stress the benefits of keeping the ball on the ground. Balls on the ground are easier to handle by teammates and are unlikely to promote collisions between the head and other hard objects.

On rare occasions concussions may be caused when a player is unexpectedly struck in the head by the ball. Teach players that when defenders are under pressure, they often resort to trying to blast the ball clear. If players are alert and ready, they may be able to avoid being hit in the head from close range.

Teaching the Header Pass

Simple heading is often an effective way to make short passes to a team-mate, especially back to the goalkeeper (who is allowed to handle a headed ball but not a pass from feet).

Confident Coaching Tips for the Header Pass

1. Keep chin and neck muscles locked to prevent unnecessary jar-ring of the head on impact.

Step-by-Step for the Header Pass

◎ Time your movement to the ball so you are positioned under the ball as it arrives.

◎ Arch your back and tense neck muscles.

Tell players to watch the ball and not to close their eyes when heading.

Explain that the power for a header comes from the body, not the neck.

◎ Meet the ball with your forehead (between the eyebrows and hairline).

◎ Provide power to the header with your body, thrusting forward from the waist—not with the neck.

◎ Follow through in the direction you want the ball to go.

Teaching the Jump Header

Learning this skill well is essential to safer heading, whether a player is clearing a dangerous cross or putting the ball into the net. Tell players that they can minimize impact to the head by using their bodies to help absorb the ball's impact. Minimize the number of repetitions with real balls during training. Instead, work on timing using lightweight balls.

Confident Coaching Tips for the Jump Header

1. To win head balls, get to a spot where the ball can be headed before your opponent does. If that is not possible, desist and thereby avoid injury to opponents and yourself.

2. To get more height to your jump, bend your knees and push off with both feet. Swing your arms forward at liftoff.

3. During your jump, keep your eyes opened and focused on the ball.

Safety tip: Teach players to beware of dangerous heading situations that can result in concussions. For example, players will often "help" a weak clearance or service into the goal area by flicking it backward with their head. Typically, they do not know if there is an opponent behind them also trying to reach the ball. By recognizing the dangers of such situations, players may take precautions, such as glancing back before heading the ball. Tell players that when they are "behind" the header to keep a safe distance.

Step-by-Step for Taking the Jump Header

○ Time your approach so the ball will fall slightly in front of you.

○ Jump to meet the ball, keeping your chin tucked in and neck muscles locked.

○ Arch your back with arms and elbows out and shoulders and knees back. Your body should look like a bow.

○ For distance and height (when clearing), hit the ball just below the middle. Follow through forward and upward for distance and height.

○ For shooting hit the ball in the middle and drive it forward or downward.

Heading Games to Use in Practice

Head to Feet—Similar to "Under the Bridge" (page 62), this game is a gentle way to become familiar with proper heading techniques. Divide players into groups of three. Ask one player to stand between the other two and to spread his legs wide. The two remaining players take turns heading the ball to each other, through the legs of their partner. When one player makes five successful passes, he moves to the center and the game continues. Vary distances depending on the age and skill level of the players.

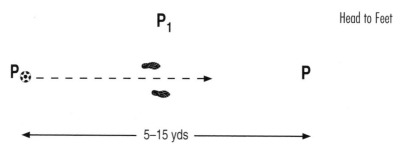

Head to Feet

Soccer Volleyball—Encourage small groups of players to toss the ball in the air and to try to keep it there. For younger players two or three touches in the air are all you should expect. Ask older players to attempt five or six continuous passes. Once players become proficient, set up a volleyball court using cones (or use the center circle). Tie a string about 4 feet high between corner flags for the net—or go without a net and say the ball simply has to cross the center line in the air. You may restrict the game to heading only, with only the service being tossed. Or, you may allow the head and foot to be used. If doing the latter, you may allow the ball to bounce once per side in order to produce longer rallies.

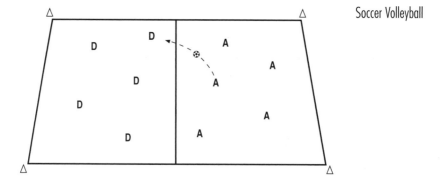

Soccer Volleyball

CHAPTER 14

TEACHING THROWING

Throwing involves both body mechanics and rules of the game. It is generally good to teach both at once. All throw-ins must occur with both feet behind or on the sideline. Hands must grasp the ball at the sides, not behind. The ball must be withdrawn behind the head and then thrown forward in a straight continuous motion—no last instant twists or turns! Feet must not lift off the ground.

Teaching the Short Throw-in

For younger players focus on the simple short throw. Explain that for a throw to be successful, it takes two: the thrower and the receiver. The thrower must deliver the ball, but the receiver is responsible for becoming open to receive it. It's OK for the thrower to yell the receiver's name, although after playing together for a while all that's needed is a nod or look.

Confident Coaching Tips for the Short Throw-in

1. By turning to face your target receiver at the last second, you will make it easier for your teammates to become open.

2. Make short throws to a teammate's feet. It will make it easier for him to play the ball.

3. Becoming open for a throw often requires the help of teammates. Explain that by having several players moving toward and away

from the thrower gives the thrower more targets. Making a run up the sideline, for example, may draw a defender away from the throw-in area, allowing another teammate to be open for the throw.

Step-by-Step for Making the Short Throw-in

- ○ Grasp the sides of the ball with both hands.
- ○ Stand a few feet from the line and look for possible teammates to receive the throw.
- ○ Step to the line (but not over it) and raise the ball behind your head.

Stress that players use their whole body when throwing, not just the arms.

- ○ Turn to face your intended target and throw the ball in a continuous motion.

Teaching the Long Throw

Long throws come into play once players reach nine or ten years old, as these throws require more coordination and strength. They are similar to short throws but involve techniques for developing more power and distance.

Confident Coaching Tips for the Long Throw

1. Tell players to grip the ball strongly with the index fingers behind the ball and the rest of the fingers holding the ball's sides.

2.   For maximum power players should extend their arms as far behind their body as possible before throwing the ball. It also helps to bend the knees slightly, arch the back, and flex elbows and wrists backward.

3.   For added distance the wrists should flip forward on release of the ball.

Step-by-Step for Making the Long Throw

○   Grasp the sides of the ball with both hands, fingers spread.

○   Run toward the side touchline.

○   Bring the ball over your head and behind your neck as your approach the line. Bend back elbows and wrists.

Snapping the wrists upon releasing the ball will allow players to make longer throws.

○   Throw the ball forward, snapping wrists forward and fully extending your arms on release. Your feet can end up together or one in front of the other.

○   Follow through with both hands swinging forward.

Throw-in Games to Use in Practice

Target Toss—Have players pair up and stand about 10 to 30 yards apart. Make a small goal with two cones. Have players alternate throwing the ball through the goal, focusing on making proper throws and accuracy. Lengthen the distance between players as they improve and ask them to throw with greater pace.

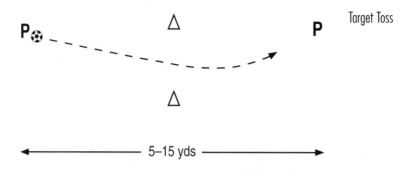

Target Toss

Throw Strengtheners—To build throwing muscles and to master technique, have players pair up, one ball per pair. Ask the player with the ball to lie on her back and extend the ball behind her back. On your signal ask her to do a sit-up and throw the ball to a partner—who in turn takes a try. Continue until each player has made ten to fifteen throws. You may also try this exercise with the throwing players beginning on their knees. Have them bring the ball behind their back and toward the ground as far as they can. Then ask them to snap their body forward, make the throw, and land on their hands.

CHAPTER 15

FAKES
AND MOVES

Moves are a fun part of the game and should be taught at a young age. They are very helpful for freeing players for a shot and for creating goal-scoring opportunities. We'll offer instructions for two of the most basic—and useful. Players can learn many other moves. For a complete manual on 1 versus 1 moves, see *Make Your Move* by Alfred Galustian and Charlie Cooke.

Teaching the Cut

The cut is probably the simplest of all moves to learn. It can be used in a wide variety of situations, including eluding an oncoming or chasing defender. The deception is based on quickly and unexpectedly changing the direction the player and ball are traveling.

Confident Coaching Tips for the Cut

1. Encourage players to learn to make the cut with either foot.

2. Cuts should be made away from the nearest defender and the dribbler's body should be placed in a way that shields (protects) the ball.

Step-by-Step for Making the Cut Move

- ◎ Tap the ball forward and accelerate toward it.
- ◎ Cut (stop) the ball with the outside or inside of your foot and turn it away from the nearest defender.

a. Approach the ball as if to kick it . . .   b. but stop short and . . .   c. cut the ball in a new direction.

- ◎ Pivot away from the defender and accelerate with the ball in a new direction. Alternatively, prepare the ball for a pass.

Teaching the Step Over

The step over is effective because many defenders take their cues from the movement of the body not the ball. The deception occurs when a player pretends to kick the ball or to move in a direction—but doesn't.

Confident Coaching Tips for the Step Over

1. Once again, players should learn to execute with either foot.
2. Teach your players to be good actors. When faking a kick, have them put energy into it. When faking a run, they should turn the whole body in that direction.
3. After making a move, accelerate away quickly. Otherwise, a defender will quickly recover.

Step-by-Step for Making the Step Over Move

◐ Moving to a defender, lean away from the direction in which you ultimately plan to move the ball, or retract your leg as if you intend to kick the ball.

◐ Step over (or slightly behind) the ball instead of continuing to dribble or instead of kicking it.

◐ Plant your step-over foot; quickly pivot away from the defender.

◐ Then push the ball away from the defender with your step-over foot and accelerate away.

Tell players to approach the defender at half speed before stepping over the ball and leaning away from the direction they want to go.

They should then use the opposite foot to push the ball past the defender before accelerating away at full speed.

Move Games to Use in Practice

1 versus 1 Challenge—An effective game for mastering moves is to make a grid (box) with four cones for each pair of players. Place the cones about 20 yards apart. Players begin at either end of the box, one with the ball. The player with the ball approaches the defending player and attempts to use a move in dribbling by him through the opposite pair of cones. After five attempts, change roles.

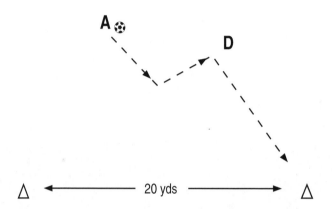

1 versus 1 Challenge

Move and Pass—Set two targets, such as large cones, 15 to 20 yards apart. Two players face off between the targets. The one with the ball tries to move past the other and immediately passes the ball at the target. Score one point each time a player uses a move successfully and one point if the target is hit.

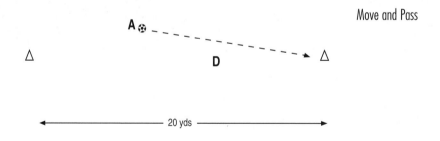

Move and Pass

Part III
GOALKEEPING

CHAPTER 16

GOALKEEPING— AN INTRODUCTION

Youth soccer coaches often neglect teaching goalkeeping. Most are unfamiliar with the skills and barely have time to teach field skills before the next match rolls around. In addition many coaches feel that because goalkeeping involves catching and throwing the ball, skills most American kids seem born with, special training is not necessary.

This is untrue and unfortunate for players who are thrust into the position without training. Successful goalkeeping requires specialized training. It is also critical to the success of your team. A match often depends on a single save. It therefore makes sense to devote several practices per season to teaching goalkeeping skills. Your keepers will benefit—and so will field players who will be able to see the field and how play develops from the keeper's vantage.

Goalkeeping, unlike other positions in soccer, has its own set of skills. They fall into two basic categories: making saves and distributing the ball. Making saves includes knowing where to position yourself in various situations, how to stand in the ready stance, the most efficient ways to step to the ball, how to handle the ball when it gets to you (catch, punch, or parry), and how to protect yourself from injury. Distribution is what you do once you have made a save. It includes deciding when and from where to release the ball, to whom, and by what method (throw or kick).

Field skills are important for goalkeepers to have, as well. Rule changes in recent years have required keepers to become better at dribbling, receiving, and passing. No longer can they scoop up a pass kicked from a teammate with their hands. They must play such balls with their feet—often in the face of pressure from opposing attackers. Keepers are also often responsible for taking goal kicks.

Finally, a keeper must be a good communicator. Keepers are often in the best position to call out information about what is happening on the field because they have a view of the entire field. For example, if a keeper knows she can be first to the ball, she should shout, "Keeper." If free to receive a pass from a pressured defender, she yells, "Back." If it is clear that the defender cannot turn from pressure, the correct call is, "Clear it!" In free kick situations keepers must quickly help position defensive walls to reduce the chance for a goal to be scored. Similarly, goalkeepers will organize their defenders in corner kick situations, ensuring that both posts are covered and that all attackers are marked (covered).

CHAPTER 17

TEACHING
THE STANCE

The first thing to teach young goalkeepers is the "ready stance." It will allow them to react quickly and to move in any direction in order to save a shot.

Confident Coaching Tips for Teaching the Ready Stance

1. When assuming the ready stance, stay loose and relaxed, not stiff and tense.

2. Rest your weight on the balls of your feet, heels raised and toes pointing out.

The ready stance allows players to react to shots quickly.

Step-by-Step for the Ready Stance

O   Raise head but keep neck muscles relaxed. Keep eyes on the ball.

O   Position arms in front of the body. Bend elbows so that the forearms are parallel to the ground.

O   Raise hands above elbows, palms down, and extend them forward.

O   Bend body forward so that shoulders are in front of the feet.

O   Bend knees slightly and slightly spread feet.

CHAPTER 18

CATCHING THE BALL

Key elements to being a good keeper are getting the body in front of the shot and having good hand position. While the former is a matter of anticipation and quickness, the latter is determined by the placement of the shot.

Teaching the Basic Contour Catch

To catch a ball that is chest high or higher, use the contour catch. With this hand position, you will be able to block the ball even when you are unable to catch it cleanly.

Confident Coaching Tips for the Contour Catch

1. Flex wrists forward and extend arms slightly outward in order to absorb some of the impact of the ball and to make catching it easier.

2. Use two hands equally to make the catch. Once caught, cover the ball with hands and arms to keep from dropping it, especially when making a save in traffic.

Step-by-Step for Making the Basic Contour Catch

◐ Move in front of the oncoming ball and raise your hands to catch the ball.

O Cup your hands so they are in the shape of the ball and position them thumb to thumb.

O Catch the ball and bring it to your chest.

The thumb-to-thumb hands position is the key to all contour catches.

Teaching the High Contour Catch

The high contour catch is for balls that are played higher than you can reach without jumping. It is especially useful for catching crossing and corner kicks played across the box.

Confident Coaching Tips for the High Contour Catch

1. Thrust one knee upward for extra lift and to protect yourself from onrushing attackers.

2. Be sure to pull the ball to your body, protecting it with hands and arms, to prevent it from bouncing free in a collision.

Step-by-Step for Making the High Contour Catch

O Move quickly so you face the oncoming ball, raise your arms, and leap from one foot.

O Position your hands as for the basic contour catch and make the catch.

Teaching the Side Contour Catch

The side contour catch is for balls shot to either side of you, that you cannot get in front of.

Confident Coaching Tips for the Side Contour Catch

1. When you attempt to save a ball while you are moving, there is a much greater chance of dropping it. Be prepared to fall on a dropped ball if necessary.

Step-by-Step for Making the Side Contour Catch

◖ Move quickly toward the ball and extend your arms into its path.

◖ Position your hands thumb to thumb and cupped as for the basic contour catch.

Tell keepers to immediately hug the ball to their chest upon making the side contour catch.

◖ Make the catch with one hand behind the top of the ball and the other behind the bottom of it.

Teaching the Basket Catch

The basket catch is used for catching balls that come below chest height.

Confident Coaching Tips for the Basket Catch

1. After catching the ball, bend your upper body forward to cover the ball and lessen the chance of it rebounding into play.

Step-by-Step for Making the Basket Catch

- Move quickly so you face the oncoming ball.
- Lower your hands into the path of the ball, arms extended.

a. Tell keepers to extend arms away from body when making a basket catch.

b. They should then cradle the ball to prevent it from popping loose.

- Position your hands, little finger to little finger.
- Bend at the waist as the ball reaches you and form a basket with your hands and arms.

Catching Games to Use in Practice

Keeper Catch (for basic contour catch and all other types of catches)— Have players pair up and face off at a distance of about 5 yards. Have them take turns throwing the ball above chest height to each other. See how many catches each player can make without dropping the ball. After every ten completions, each player takes a long step backward. Use the same game for the high, side, and basket catches, making the appropriately placed throws.

CHAPTER 19

DISTRIBUTING
THE BALL

Making saves is what makes a keeper valuable, but knowing what to do with the ball afterward is nearly as important. Teach your players that it's everyone's job to maintain possession after the keeper makes a save. Field players should get open in order to be a target for a pass. Keepers must pursue the safest option when turning the ball over to teammates, which usually means distribution toward the sides of the field, not the middle. Keepers have several options for passing the ball to teammates (as described in the following).

Teaching the Bowl Throw

Use the bowl throw for short, accurate passes. It is a great way for young keepers who cannot yet punt with distance or accuracy to distribute the ball.

Confident Coaching Tips for the Bowl Throw

1. Point your front foot toes toward your target.
2. Smoothly "lay" the ball on the ground (as in bowling) so it does not bounce and is easy for your teammate to receive.

Step-by-Step for Making the Bowl Throw

○ Hold the ball in front of you as you step in the direction you want to throw it.

When teaching the bowl throw, show keepers how to balance the ball between the palm and forearm. For young keepers, it's okay to steady the ball with their free hand.

○ Spread your fingers and cup the ball between your palm and forearm.

○ Bring the ball back, weight on rear foot.

○ Swing it forward and release, bending your knees.

○ Follow through with your arm in the direction you want the ball to go.

Teaching the Sling Throw

Use the sling throw to make accurate passes at medium distance.

Confident Coaching Tips for the Sling Throw

1. Point front foot toes in the direction in which you want to throw.

2. Release the ball at head height for maximum distance.

3. As you throw the ball, step forward and shift weight to your front foot. Release the ball, using your body to add power to the throw.

4. By imparting a backspin to your throw, it will be easier for your teammate to handle.

Step-by-Step for Making the Sling Throw

○ Stand parallel to the direction in which you want to throw the ball, holding the ball lightly between your palm and arm.

Teach keepers to align their bodies with the direction of the throw.

○ Bring back the ball behind your body at waist height, arching your back and balancing on your back foot.

○ Point your free arm in the direction you want to throw the ball.

○ Palm up, elbow locked, sling the ball over your head.

Teaching How to Punt

The punt is a good way to distribute the ball when opponents cut off your ability to distribute to the flanks or when a long kick will give your defenders time to reorganize.

Confident Coaching Tips for Punting

1. Strike the ball just before it reaches the ground for maximum distance.

2. If you are kicking right-footed, hold the ball in your left hand; if left-footed, hold it in your right hand.

Step-by-Step for Punting

○ Step in the direction you want to kick the ball, holding the ball in one hand if possible.

a Show keepers how to drop the ball with one hand. . .   b . . . and punt with the opposite foot.

○ Drop the ball and focus your eyes on the spot where you will kick it, slightly below its center.

○ Lock your ankle and point its toe away from your body. Then strike the ball with your instep.

○ Follow through high with your leg but keep your head down.

Games That Improve Distribution

Keeper Croquet—Set up small goals, 24 inches wide and 10 to 15 yards apart. Place the goals as you would wickets for croquet. Divide players into groups of two or three and play croquet using the bowl throw.

Target Practice—Divide players into pairs. Place tall cones about 20 to 30 yards apart and position players behind the cones. Ask each player to use the sling throw or bowl throw to try to hit the cone. Vary the distance depending on the age and skill of the players.

Punting Challenge—Have players pair up and take turns punting to each

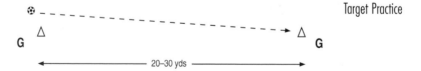

Target Practice

20–30 yds

other. The first player marks the spot from which she kicks with a T-shirt. The second marks the spot where the first punt lands and makes her punt from there. If she can punt past the first punter's starting spot, she wins a point. If not, the point goes to the first punter. Continue in sets of ten. If it becomes obvious that one player is dominant, allow the weaker punter a handicap of several yards.

CHAPTER 20

MAKING DIFFICULT SAVES

As any keeper quickly learns, it is not always possible to catch a shot without leaving your feet. And sometimes it's not possible to catch the shot at all. Here are some skills keepers need to handle these situations.

Teaching Parrying

The parry is an option when you cannot catch the ball, such as when the shot is too hard and/or out of reach. It is also useful for young kids whose hands are often not large or strong enough to catch the ball.

Confident Coaching Tips for Parrying

1. You may choose to parry in any number of directions: down where you can pick it up, up and over the crossbar, up where you can catch it, or in pressure situations, as wide as possible.

2. If you want the parry to land near you, pull your hands back at contact to cushion the impact. If you want the ball to travel some distance, stiffen your arm as the ball strikes the heel of your hand.

3. Keep fingers together to avoid sprains should you misjudge a parry. In high-pressure situations, where you must dive to make the save, try to parry the ball around the goalpost and out of play.

Step-by-Step for Parrying

○   Reach toward the middle of the oncoming ball.

○   Extend your arm or arms in the direction you want the ball to go and punch it with the heel or heels of your hands.

Tell keepers to parry the ball only in situations where they cannot catch it.

Teaching Tipping

For high shots that cannot be reached with both hands, whether driven or looping over a keeper's head, tipping is often useful. When tipping, a keeper uses her fingers to direct the ball over the crossbar.

Confident Coaching Tips for Tipping

1.   This technique is best used on soft shots. Use the parry, if possible, for hard shots.

2.   When outside the 6-yard box, instruct keepers to tip the ball high and wide.

3.   Train keepers to be able to tip with either hand.

Step-by-Step for Tipping

○   Turn sideways to the goal and use shuffle steps to move toward the shot. (This means you will tip with your left hand when moving to your right, and with your right when moving to your left.)

○   Keep your eyes on the bottom panel of the ball, which is where you will want to make contact.

- Push off with the leg that is opposite to the tipping arm. Pump your other leg toward the ball.

- With fingers stiff and pushing with your shoulder and elbow, guide the ball safely over the crossbar.

Teaching the Collapse Dive

The collapse dive is for balls that you cannot quite reach and still stay on your feet. Unlike the full extension dive, however, you are never completely airborne.

Confident Coaching Tips for the Collapse Dive

1. Don't use the collapse dive if you can move in front of the ball and make the save without diving. By making saves look as easy and you can, you will build the confidence of your teammates and demoralize your opponents.

2. Try to control your fall to the ground. Do not flop or the ball will likely be jarred loose.

3. Catch the ball away from your face to protect yourself from being kicked in the head.

Step-by-Step for Making the Collapse Dive

- Stride forward to meet the shot, keeping both legs in contact with the ground and your eyes focused on the ball.

- Extend your body as necessary to catch the ball, using the side contour catch (one hand behind and one on top of the ball).

The ball can be used by keepers to cushion their fall after a dive.

○   As you fall, "place" the ball onto the ground in front of you to help cushion your landing. Bend your knees and raise your legs slightly.

○   Pull the ball to your chest and roll away from danger to protect your head from being kicked after you have made the save.

Teaching the Sliding Save

Use the sliding save to win balls that you can reach before the shooter can.

Confident Coaching Tips for the Sliding Save

1.   Focus on the ball not the striker.

2.   Position your body so it blocks as much of the goal as possible.

3.   On making the catch protect yourself by pulling your knees up and in toward your body.

Step-by-Step for Making the Sliding Save

○   Approach the ball hard with your body low. Then drop to your side and slide toward the ball.

○   Extend your hands toward the ball and away from your face.

○   Catch the ball and pull it to your chest.

Teaching the Reaction Save

Use the reaction save to stop breakaways when you cannot beat the shooter to the ball.

Confident Coaching Tips for the Reaction Save

1.   Be ready to react should the attacker decide to pass instead of shoot.

2.   If you are unable to catch the ball cleanly, be prepared to get up quickly and pick it up—or if it is nearby, to cover it.

Step-by-Step for Making the Reaction Save

○   Move out from the goal straight toward the ball, keeping your eyes focused on it.

○ Remain standing to obscure as much of the goal as possible.

○ Lean slightly forward, hands down and palms out.

○ Make the catch using the appropriate hand positions and the collapse dive if necessary.

Games That Improve Keeper Reactions

Parry Challenge—Two or more players parry the ball to each other and see how many times they can do it without the ball hitting the ground. Devise various challenges to make the game more interesting. For instance, try parrying while sitting on the ground or while moving.

Tipping Challenge—Two or more players tip the ball to each other. Tell them to focus on technique, as described here, alternating hands, jumping for height, and pushing the ball with stiff fingers.

Catch and Collapse—Divide players into pairs and ask them to kneel, facing each other 2 or 3 yards apart. Ask them to toss the ball back and forth, first to the left, and then, right. The receiving player catches the ball using the side contour catch and then collapses with the ball.

Face-Off (for practicing sliding, collapse dive, and reaction saves)— Divide players into pairs and make two goals with cones from about 20 to 25 yards apart for each pair. Ask the players to take turns dribbling toward each other and to either attempt to dribble into the goal or to shoot from about 5 yards away. The defending player makes a sliding save, collapse dive save, or a reaction save. Advise players to dribble and shoot at half speed to start. This will allow their partners to concentrate on technique without worrying about getting hurt.

PK Baseball—Divide players into threes, make a goal for each group with cones, and mark a penalty spot about 12 yards away. Ask one player from each group be the ball retriever. Designate one as the PK taker and one as the keeper. Ask the PK taker to begin taking penalty kicks, with a PK being a "run" and a miss being an out. After three outs, rotate. The winner is the player with the most runs after six innings. If not playing with real goals, add a rule that permits goals only if scored under knee level. Balls shot into the goal that are higher than the knees may be counted as foul balls.

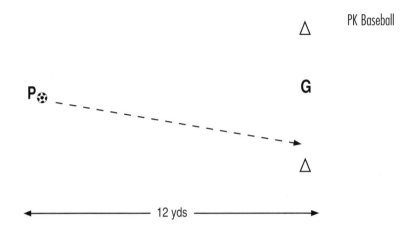

PK Baseball

12 yds

Battling Keepers (for practicing all kinds of saves and improving reaction time)—Divide your players into two teams of keepers. Move and re-anchor goals so they are about 50 feet apart. Gather half your balls (at least eight) beside one goal and half beside the other. Then ask one keeper from each team to step into goal. On your signal these keepers must try to throw or kick as many of their balls as possible into their opponents' net. When a goal is scored, a new keeper enters the goal as quickly as possible. If a goal is scored during the transition, it counts but the new keeper does not have to leave the goal. The first team to score twenty-one goals wins.

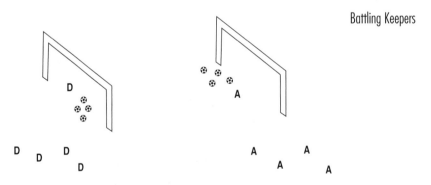

Battling Keepers

Advanced Goalkeeping Skills

Teaching more advanced goalkeeper skills, such as extension dives and smother saves, may be beyond the capability of most parent coaches. If your team's keepers are interested in learning more, let them know about goalkeeper clinics and soccer camps in your area. Many youth soccer clubs organize clinics for goalkeepers, knowing that most coaches have little or no training in the position. They usually feature a goalkeeper coach from a nearby college. Sometimes the club will pay the fee and in other cases parents will be asked to contribute a nominal amount. Specialized goalkeeper camps for kids are also available. Usually a part of a general soccer camp, goalkeepers receive training separately during part of the day and then have the opportunity to put their skills to the test during matches with field players.

Part IV
PUTTING IT ALL TOGETHER

CHAPTER 21

POSITIONS AND FORMATIONS

It may seem odd to be more than halfway through a book on coaching before mentioning anything about player positions. However, with soccer it is not. Positions are far less important in "the beautiful game," as Pelé the Brazilian superstar called it, than in many other sports. Perhaps it is because once the play begins, it is the players who must make decisions about what they should do—not coaches. The game is far too complex and fluid for a coach to insist on hard-and-fast positions, such as in baseball or American football. The roles of players are continually shifting in soccer, so much so that at one moment an attacking player may be attempting to score and thirty seconds later may be heading the ball away from his own goal. Nevertheless, it is important for coaches and players to understand positions and to become familiar with the various approaches to deploying players, called formations.

Teaching Positions

It is helpful to teach young players the proper names for the positions, to show where they line up at the start of play, and to describe their roles. If the players have already been introduced to more structured sports, such as baseball, remind them that soccer positions are not so strict. In fact, players should be encouraged to react to the ever-changing flow of the game.

Starting Positions

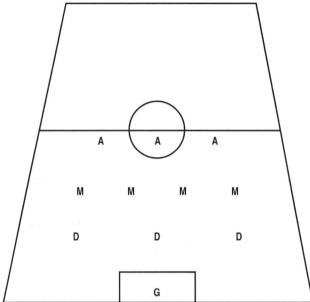

A simple diagram, written on a handheld erasable chalkboard, is a good way to introduce the positions. Later, it can be used to describe the zone of primary responsibility for each player. Two-dimensional diagrams, however, may not be enough. Remember that every person has a unique way of learning. So reinforce the diagrams with demonstrations on the field. You can try interactive demonstrations, such as placing players in their positions and asking them to shout out the position name. If young players are having a hard time with this, use cones to locate the position starting points. You can even label the cones with a marker.

As this can quickly become boring for kids, do not try to do it all in the first practice session. You can come back to it as many times as necessary. Be creative as well. For example, when teaching the starting points for positions, turn the demonstration into a gigantic game of musical chairs: tell players to move from position starting point to position starting point, shouting the name of the position as they get there. On your signal, such as a whistle blow, they must return to their original position.

Once starting points are mastered, ask each player to roam through their position's area of responsibility. Encourage them to stretch the zones far and wide—as shown in the diagrams—but to always be aware of their primary responsibilities.

If you are coaching a team that plays small-sided soccer, your job is relatively easy as the positions are probably limited to left and/or right attacker, left and/or right defender, and perhaps a goalkeeper. As kids become older and graduate from 3 versus 3 to 6 versus 6 or 8 versus 8 and finally to 11 versus 11 positions are refined. With older kids, especially those who are beginners, be sure to review both the starting points and each position's area of responsibility. You do not want new players to lose interest due to confusion about positions.

A good way to review positions with older players is to use the "whistle and freeze" approach. Divide your squad into two groups. Distribute training vests so the teams are obvious. Then assign positions for each player. Toss a ball toward one goal or the other and ask players to react. After a few seconds blow your whistle and tell them to freeze. Then quickly assess everyone's position. This is best done on half a field or less or you will shout yourself hoarse. If everyone has converged on the ball, explain that it gives the ball-possessing team far fewer passing options. If the central defender is the first to the ball in the opponent's half, ask if this will leave her goal unprotected in the

POSITIONS FOR FULL-SIDED (11v11) SOCCER

Center forward

- Key skills: Dribbling, shooting, one-touch passing, turning, 1versus1 moves.
- Key attributes: Quickness, timing, courage, and creativity.
- Primary duties: Score goals.

Outside forwards

- Key skills: Shooting, crosses, and corner kicks; one-touch passing; 1versus1 moves.
- Key attributes: Speed and timing.
- Primary duties: Assist in the scoring of goals.

Center midfielder

- Key skills: Receiving, dribbling, passing, chipping, long shots, 1versus1 moves.
- Key attributes: Vision, quickness, leadership.
- Primary duties: Distribute ball to players who penetrate, assist on offense and defense.

POSITIONS FOR FULL-SIDED (11v11) SOCCER

continued...

Outside midfielders

- Key skills: Passing, long shots and crosses, throwing.
- Key attributes: Speed, endurance.
- Primary duties: Help move ball from defense to attack, assist on offense and defense, open field by being a passing option for defenders, midfielders, and forwards.

Central defenders

- Key skills: Tackling, passing, heading, long passes, and clearing.
- Key attributes: Strength, speed, endurance, stability, determination.
- Primary duties: Stop penetration by attackers, pass ball to open midfielders, goal kicks.

Outside defenders

- Key skills: Tackling, long passes and clearing, throwing.
- Key attributes: Strength, speed, endurance, stability.
- Primary duties: Keep attackers from penetrating center of field, pass ball to open midfielders, open up the field by being a safe outside passing option for goalkeepers and central defenders.

Goalkeeper

- Key skills: Catching, diving, throwing, punting, long kicks, receiving.
- Key attributes: Strength, good hands, jumping ability, courage, good communication, concentration.
- Primary duties: Save balls from entering the net; organize the defense, especially for free kicks; goal kicks; initiate attacks with intelligent ball distribution.

event of a counterattack. If the squad without the ball is not providing pressure or not marking, explain that they are unlikely to score if they do not have the ball. Get your players involved in the discussion. Ask questions such as: Are you helping the team by being where you are? Is

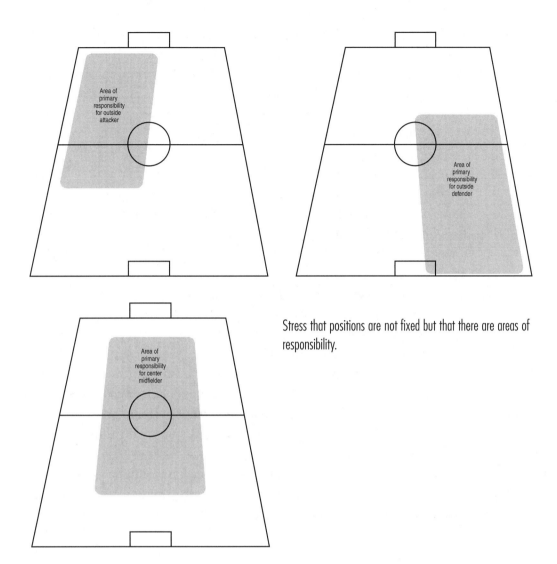

Stress that positions are not fixed but that there are areas of responsibility.

there a better place to be? Is there a way to cover for a teammate who is missing from where she should be? You will be able to use this teaching technique for teaching tactics, as well.

Understanding Formations

Before your team even begins to play eleven-a-side soccer, most coaches will have heard about soccer formations. These are time-tested ways to deploy players to best advantage. One formation may be favored over another based on the strengths and weaknesses of the team or the strengths and weaknesses of an opposing team. Or they may be determined by a coach's preferred system of play.

Formations are identified by number sequences, such as 4-4-2 and 3-4-3. The first number refers to the number of defenders; the second, midfielders; and the third, forwards or attackers. The numbers are always listed from defense to offense, so a 4-3-3 means there are four defenders, three midfielders, and three forwards. Since there is always one goalkeeper, they are not included in the designations.

The most common formations in youth soccer are 4-3-3 at the younger ages and 4-4-2 at older ages.

For youth coaches formations are often used to shade play toward how offensive or defensive you want your team to play. A coach who feels his team is outmatched, for example, may choose a more defensive formation, such as a 4-4-2, or even a 4-5-1. A coach who is playing against a weak team may choose a 2-3-5.

Formations go in and out of style. When I played in high school, the almost universal formation was 2-3-5. Our five attackers were center, right, and left inners, and right and left outers. Early versions of the game relied on a 9-1 formation!

The numbers do not tell the whole story. A 4-4-2, for instance, may be made up of left and right defenders, a stopper (first man to the ball on defense), and a sweeper (last man on defense). On the other hand, the same formation may have a flat or level back four, with four defenders each responsible for their areas.

With young children it is not wise to put much emphasis on formations. If a child understands she needs to pay attention to a particular side of the field on attack or defense, it is enough.

CHAPTER 22

TEACHING TACTICS

At its most simple, the object of soccer is to put the ball into your opponent's net and to keep it out of yours. Tactics are what you use to accomplish this object. With good tactics players create opportunities to score goals—and deny their opponents the same opportunities.

Ultimately, tactics drive a child's desire to learn the sport. They are the most challenging part of the game. There are many other appealing aspects of the game, such as being outside with friends, getting exercise, and so on, but tactics are what the game is about.

Many coaches will tell you that tactics cannot be taught to young kids. They feel more comfortable demonstrating skills and believe that these tools of play must be taught before a player can even begin to think about tactics.

Perhaps coaches shy away from addressing tactics with young kids because they have a "playbook" mentality and think of tactics in terms of X's and O's and wiggly arrows. Tactics are in fact the building blocks of the game, and players can begin to understand them from the first time a player tries to score a goal.

Examples of Early Tactical Thinking

Early on, players learn that it is not easy to either advance the ball or defend a goal alone, hence the most basic tactic of all: find ways to get help from your teammates. For example, the earliest "tactic" your child may try is to kick the ball forward, out of the "hive" of players around her; chase it; and kick it again at the goal. This may work in the first few matches a child plays, but she will soon discover that opponents adjust and quickly figure out how to stop the player who tries to go it alone.

Eventually, even very young players realize they must rely on teammates to help them advance the ball. Hence, a few kids come up with the clever idea of standing near the opponent's goal waiting for one of his teammates to kick the ball near him so he can score. The child who realizes this is thinking, so do not criticize him. Soon enough, he will realize this is a limited tactic. First, defensive players learn to mark (guard) the "goal hanger." Second, while the goal hanger is waiting for the ball to come to him, the players on the other team have an easier time of scoring on the opposite end of the field because they outnumber their opponents.

On defense a child's first tactic is often to retreat to the goal and to stand in front of it, hoping to block a shot. She soon realizes that this approach stops few goals—and that it is better to try to take the ball from an opponent before she reaches the goal area. Next, she discovers that trying to stop an advancing player with the help of a teammate is a lot easier than doing it alone. This leads to understanding that sometimes it is preferable to slow an opponent down in order to give a teammate time to arrive to help.

How to Teach Tactics

Tactics may be taught formally. Or, if you prefer, allow kids to discover them for themselves. My approach is to do a little of each. When I see that some children have discovered a way to advance the ball or to defend more effectively, I praise them and ask them to try to describe what they have learned. In this way they become conscious of what they have done and their teammates learn as well.

Of course, teaching tactics must be balanced with skills instruction. Tactics give kids an incentive to work on skills, while skills give kids the ability to attempt more sophisticated tactics.

When you hear a coach say the game is the best teacher, it is another way of saying that tactics are what motivates players to improve. In much of the world, kids become very skillful with very little training because they are driven to learn the skills in order to attempt more sophisticated tactics.

Tactics are best learned in small-sided games where players are challenged to think. Whether during training sessions or on game day, be sure to reward all tactical thinking with praise, even when a player's idea is not the best tactic. Do not force-feed kids with high-level tactics for which they are too young or unprepared.

Play games that require thinking to be successful, not only athleticism. During matches take note of tactical ideas demonstrated by your players. Try to talk about them afterward. For example, if one of your players discovers that roaming the goal area is a way to score goals, discuss the idea. What is good about it? Are there negatives as well? How do other players support the idea? Remember: the excitement generated by discovering a new tactic gives kids the incentive to master the relatively less exciting skills.

Tactical Guidelines

Tactics are basic rules or principles that a team agrees on. They determine how players should react in various situations and enable teams to act in unison with a single purpose. U.S. Soccer Federation coaching directors and instructors have identified general tactical principles and suggest that coaches try to instill them in their players.

There are two kinds of tactics: offensive (your team has the ball) and defensive (your team does not have the ball).

Tactics for Younger Players

For players under the age of eleven or twelve, keep your tactical suggestions simple. On offense stress the idea of "exploding" and "stretching" the field. By spreading out when a teammate wins the ball, the team creates passing opportunities. Conversely, on defense the team should "implode" or "shrink" to the area on the field between the ball and the goal being defended.

Other key tactical guidelines for younger players include the following:

Rely primarily on passing to move the ball forward. A fun way to demonstrate the effectiveness of passing is to ask your team who is the fastest on the field. Then ask the player or players who claim to be fast to line up as if for a race. Signal go and kick a ball toward the finish line. Then point out that as fast as they are, they are a lot slower than the ball.

Follow the passes you make. After they make a pass, tell players that they should not just stand there admiring it! Remind them to run to a new place to give their teammates new passing opportunities.

Give your teammates helpful information. Coaches often admonish their players to talk. That's great, but be specific. Tell them that with every pass, they should give the receiving teammate information. If there is a player closing down on the player with the ball, the "talking" teammate will yell, "Man on." If there is no pressure, the call would be "turn," indicating that the receiver has time to turn and face the opponent's goal. "Hold" can be used to indicate that a supporting player is about to make an overlapping run. In addition players can use phrases such as "square," "on your left," "open," or "through" to give the player with the ball information about where to pass the ball and to whom.

Speed the attack when you outnumber defenders. Called having numbers, or numbers up, this is the time players should move quickly to try to score. When outnumbered by defenders or numbers down, tell your players that it is often wise to slow the attack.

Support the man with the ball. Players generally do not have much time to make a pass before coming under pressure. Your team will have far more success if they learn to "get open" for passes. Tell players to move constantly in order to be in view of the passer. If players are unable to get open due to persistent defenders, they should run away from the play to draw defenders away and create open spaces for other potential receivers.

Pressure the ball. When on defense tell players to get in front of the attacker with the ball and to slow his progress. Defenders who arrive later should support the first defender by cutting off passing angles and by being ready to grab balls that pop loose after a tackle. Once again, encourage talking. "I've got man," and "I've got ball" are useful exchanges in defensive situations.

Mark open players. Get your players in the habit of always looking to make themselves useful on defense. If they are not involved with immediate pressure on the ball, they should mark, or cover, any attackers who are likely to receive a pass.

Offensive Tactical Guidelines for Older Players

For players aged eleven and older, tactical guidelines can become more detailed. On offense a team strives for penetration into its opponents' half with *depth, width, mobility,* and *finishing.* Depth means supporting the player with the ball in front and behind. Width means supporting to the side (square) and to the flanks (sidelines). Mobility involves players making runs to exploit openings or imbalances in the opponent's defense. Finishing simply means getting the ball into the net.

For young players—and even for many older players—tactical principles are abstract and need to be translated into guidelines for how to act in specific situations.

On offense I explain to players that there are three basic possibilities: You have the ball, you are near a teammate who has the ball, or you are not near the ball. In each case there is a decision-making process that should become second nature to players.

When a player has the ball (called being the first attacker), he should:
1. Look to score.
2. Move the ball to a spot where scoring is possible (penetrate), either by dribbling or passing to a teammate who is moving to the goal.
3. Maintain possession by playing the ball away from pressure to a supporting teammate.

When near a teammate who has the ball (called being the second attacker, of which there can be more than one), she should:
1. Move to a position where she can receive a pass and score a goal.
2. Lessen the pressure on the player with the ball by making herself available for a pass to the side, front, behind, or by positioning herself for a wall pass (give-and-go).
3. Combine with the first attacker to penetrate by making runs to confuse and surprise the opposition, such as check (moving toward and then away from the passer), diagonal (through), or overlapping runs or takeovers.

When not near the ball (called being the third attacker, of which there should be several), players should:

1. Open space by drawing off a defender with a longer run, thereby creating space into which another teammate may move to receive a pass.

2. Run to an open area where you may receive a long pass that "changes the field" (moves play unexpectedly from one side of the field to the other).

3. Rotate to a defensive position to cover for a defender who has become involved in the attack.

Defensive Tactical Guidelines for Older Players

On defense the tactic is to try to regain possession as quickly as possible but without risking a goal-scoring opportunity. To do so, players give immediate chase and delay the attacking team with depth, balance, and concentration. Immediate chase means to quickly close down on the player with the ball and slow his progress. Depth, here, means to move into defensive positions in front and in back of the attacking players. Balance means to mark or cover players away from the ball who are in a position to penetrate. Concentration, or compactness, is achieved when the attacker's options have been limited or eliminated, allowing defenders to tackle, intercept, or win a loose ball.

When explaining these principles to players, it is helpful to break them down into rules. Once again, there are three possibilities:

When a player is nearest to the opponent with the ball (called being the first defender), she should:

1. Immediately get goal side (between the attacker and your goal) and delay the attacking player from advancing.

2. Deny penetration, especially to the center of the field. (Try to channel [move] the attacker to the outside.)

3. When support arrives, apply pressure and win the ball with a tackle if possible.

When near the ball, but not the closest player (second defender, of which there can be several):

1. Support the teammate who is trying to get the ball back.

2. Eliminate the attacker's best passing option.

Here, the player on the left has applied pressure and won the ball with a clean tackle.

When you are not near the player with the ball (third defenders are the remaining players):

1. Move to a place where your defense is weak, especially if it is in the center of the field.

2. Cover or mark opponents who make runs into attacking positions.

KEY TACTICAL CONCEPTS

On offense:

• Use simple passes with high probability of completion throughout most of the field. Keep dribbling to a minimum, especially in your defensive zone.

• Near the goal, it is OK to dribble or try a risky pass if necessary to surprise opponents and create a scoring opportunity.

• Dominate time of possession and there is a better chance to score. It is also less likely your team will be scored on. Short passes are the best way to maintain possession.

• Use long passes to vary the attack, surprise opponents, and tap into exceptional speed.

KEY TACTICAL CONCEPTS

continued...

- Move the ball away from pressure to open areas as you attempt to penetrate.
- Get one or more players with the ball behind your opponent's defenders to create scoring opportunities.
- Use teammates who have exceptional skill. For example, get the ball to the player who has the best chance to score. Alternatively, get the ball to the player who can "hold" the ball and make dangerous passes.
- Do not waste restarts. Take corner kicks, indirect, and direct free kicks quickly and with a plan.
- Once it is clear the ball will turn over, switch to defense. A delay of even one or two seconds can make a big difference.

On defense:
- Have more defenders between the ball and the goal (do not be outnumbered when opponents attack).
- Try to channel (move) the attacker with the ball away from the center of the field.
- Build out of the back (move the ball through the defensive third) by playing the ball to the flanks (outside) and then up field.
- Clear the ball from the goal area by kicking it as high, wide, and deep as possible.
- Under dangerous pressure, it is OK to kick the ball out of play.
- Initiate attack immediately on winning a turnover.
- Work with your goalkeeper to build defensive walls. Defend threatening restarts quickly and with purpose.

CHAPTER 23

GOALKEEPING TACTICS

It is beyond the scope of this book to cover goalkeeping tactics in depth, but there are a few tactical questions that will come up as soon as most kids play the position: where to stand when expecting a shot, how far to come out, and where to play the ball once the save has been made.

Where to stand is largely determined by the position of the potential shooter. Reduce the angles from which an attacker may shoot the ball by moving toward the shooter. Doing so exposes the least amount of open goal to a shooter as possible. Coming out also puts pressure on the shooter, often forcing him to shoot before he's ready.

How far to come out is also determined by several variables, including the number of attackers and the likelihood of the attacker with the ball passing it and how much defensive support the keeper has. Generally speaking, the more defenders, the closer the keeper stays to the goal. Few or no defenders forces a keeper to come well out into the penalty box or even beyond it to either win a ball or to force the shot from as far from the goal as possible. A keeper must be careful, however, about coming out too far. If she does, it is easy for an attacker to dribble the ball around her for an easy goal or to chip the ball over her head into the net. It is a delicate balance and takes lots of experience playing the position to make good judgments.

Where to play the ball after making the save is relatively simple, especially for young players. The safest option is to throw or punt it to the flanks where teammates can play the ball forward. Teach keepers to avoid playing it to the area in front of the goal where, if stolen, will result in an easy score. In addition teach field players to be available for passes to the flanks.

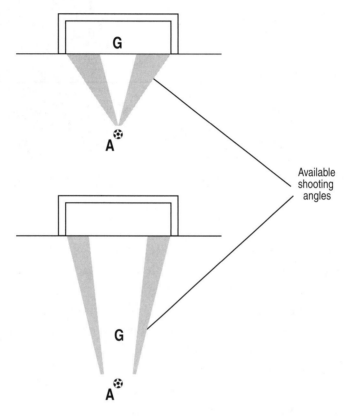

Leaving the goal to stop a breakaway reduces the shooting angles for the attacker.

Available shooting angles

CHAPTER 24

TACTICAL TOOLS TO TEACH IN PRACTICE

Many of the topics discussed in this chapter are often presented as *skills* in soccer manuals. While they all require the use of skills (usually more than one), they are more closely related to tactics.

Teaching the Give-and-Go

As one of the primary tactics is to maintain possession of the ball, teach the various ways to elude defenders. The give-and-go is the key to success in many situations. Your players may already have an understanding of it from other sports, but you should devote at least one practice session to it every season.

Confident Coaching Tips for the Give-and-Go

1. Execute the give-and-go quickly, but don't put too much pace on the ball or it will be difficult to control.

2. Deception helps, too. Do not give away your intentions by looking at your teammate as you dribble toward the defender.

3. The "go" pass should be played to your feet. With a breakaway, however, the pass may be played to open space.

Step-by-Step for the Give-and-Go

O   Dribble toward the defender at a medium pace as your team-
    mate approaches from a safe angle, one out of range of the
    defender.

O   Play the ball to your teammate's feet and run past the defender
    to the opposite side of the pass.

O   Your teammate should make a one-touch pass, with inside or
    outside of her foot, back to you.

Teaching the Overlap

The overlap takes more communication on the part of teammates but is
another great way to elude defenders and maintain possession.

Confident Coaching Tips for the Overlap

1. When a player sees the opportunity to support a teammate who
    has the ball by making an overlapping run, he should yell
    "hold" or "overlap" or some other agreed on signal.

2. This play can be used almost anywhere on the field.

Step-by-Step for the Overlap Run

O   Teammates recognize the opportunity for an overlapping run.

O   The player with the ball draws the defender away from the run.

O   The player without the ball runs past his teammate and the de-
    fender through the space created by the player with the ball.

O   The player with the ball passes the ball on the ground or in the
    air to his teammate making the run.

Teaching Checking Runs

To check away from the ball is another simple way for a potential pass
receiver to create space and time in order to receive a pass. It can be used
near the sidelines when receiving a throw in or elsewhere in the midfield.

Confident Coaching Tips for Checking Runs

1. Make a run like you mean it, as though you are going to sprint
    past the defender.

2. After successfully completing a pass to a teammate who has checked back, run to a space to create a new passing opportunity.

Step-by-Step for Making Checking Runs

○ A player who is marked runs away from his teammate with the ball, drawing the defender with her.

○ Suddenly, she turns and runs back toward the player with the ball and asks for the ball.

○ The player with the ball makes a smooth pass to the receiving player's feet, advises teammate as to whether she can turn or not, and moves to create a new passing opportunity.

Teaching about Free Kicks

The balance of a tightly fought match often hinges on how well—or poorly—a team executes its free kicks. First go over the difference between direct and indirect kicks with your players. Remind them that with a direct kick, the kick taker may shoot at the goal and score without another player touching the ball. With indirect kicks a teammate (or opposing player, but do not count on that) must touch the ball for a goal to count. Then show them several "plays" they can use during matches—and practice them frequently.

Confident Coaching Tips for Free Kicks

1. When awarded a free kick, play the ball as quickly as possible. You may catch the opposition off balance or arguing the call. Do not wait for a second whistle unless the ref asks you to.

2. If you do not have a clear shot, or if the call is for an indirect free kick, play the ball to a teammate who is near the goal.

3. If your teammates are closely marked or if you must ask the ref to push defenders back the required 10 yards, try a set play.

Step-by-Step for Free Kick Set Plays

○ This free kick set play involves three teammates. The idea is to move the ball past a wall so a shot can be taken from a better angle. The first player taps the ball to a setter, about 5 yards away. The setter stops the ball and steps back. The third player, the kicker, times his run so that he strikes the ball just after it has been stopped.

○ Several variations will enable your team to keep the opposition guessing. In the first variation, a dummy shooter runs over the ball prior to setting up the free kick as described earlier.

○ In the second variation, the setter allows the ball to pass between his legs to a fourth teammate, who takes the shot.

○ In the third variation, the passer heels the ball backward to a fourth teammate who takes the shot.

Teaching Corner Kicks

Taking corner kicks involves driving the ball into the goal area (see tips on making long passes, p. 61) as well as tactical coordination with teammates. Tell players they must try to keep the ball away from the goalkeeper and put it where a teammate can get to it first. That said, corner kicks should be delivered to one of three places: the near post, the far post, or the central goal area. The kicker should also try to time the kick so it reaches the desired spot at the same time as his teammates.

Confident Coaching Tips for Corner Kicks

1. Near-post corner kicks should be well driven so defenders do not have time to react. A teammate can then try to flick the ball on to another onrushing team member or to head it directly into the goal.

2. Far-post corner kicks should be struck high enough and wide enough to elude the keeper and with enough pace to avoid the keeper running off her line to grab it. A "floating" corner kick gives defenders time to grab it. The kick taker should aim about 8 to 10 yards out from the side of the goal, where a teammate can either shoot on goal or head the ball back across the goal area for another team member to shoot.

3. Put central corner kicks between the top of the 6-yard box and the penalty spot.

For older, more advanced players, corner kicks may be curved. Generally, an inswinging kick (one that curves toward the goal) is best. Against a tall aggressive keeper, however, an outswinging kick may be more successful. Curved kicks require the strength of a mature or nearly mature body. To curve a kick the ball must be powerfully struck with the inside or outside of the instep. The leg must pull away sharply upon contact to create enough spin for the ball to curve.

Teaching Marking

Marking simply means covering your man. Players must learn to position themselves to have the best chance of intercepting the ball when passed to the player they are marking—and the least chance of being beaten should the pass be completed.

Confident Coaching Tips for Marking

1. Stand goal side and central (behind and to the side of your man closest to the middle of the field).

2. The farther the marked player is from the player with the ball, the more you can lay off. The closer the marked player is to the ball, the closer you should mark.

Step-by-Step for Marking

○ Stand sideways to the direction of the pass so you can either run forward or backward quickly.

○ When the ball is passed to the player you are marking, first try to win it cleanly by beating her to the ball. If that is not possible, try to poke the ball away. At the very least try to prevent your opponent from turning.

Marking

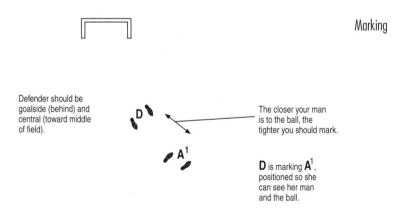

Defender should be goalside (behind) and central (toward middle of field).

The closer your man is to the ball, the tighter you should mark.

D is marking A¹, positioned so she can see her man and the ball.

Teaching Closing Down

Good defensive play often goes unrecognized because it is not spectacular. Closing down, for example, is not as dramatic as a tackle, but it is one of the ingredients to a successful team. While it simply means to move toward an opponent who has received or is about to receive the ball, it limits an opponent's passing options, especially if your teammates mark the attacking players behind you. It also makes shooting more difficult for attackers.

Confident Coaching Tips for Closing Down

1. Begin to close down as soon as it is evident that the attacking player will receive the ball or is already dribbling toward you.

Step-by-Step for Closing Down

○ If the attacker stops with the ball at his feet, close down quickly to within a foot or two.

○ If the attacker is dribbling toward you with speed, close the gap quickly but slow down as you approach to within 4 or 5 yards. Then proceed with caution and be prepared to retreat.

○ If you are near your goal or have defensive support, close down to within a foot or two.

○ If you are at midfield without defensive support, leave more room between you and the attacker.

Teaching Channeling

Channeling moves an attacker in the direction you would prefer her to go (toward your defensive strength, other defenders) and away from the goal (toward the sidelines).

Confident Coaching Tips for Channeling

1. Stay about a yard away from the attacker with your front foot roughly in line with the advancing ball. The distance will vary depending on the speed of the attacker. You must develop judgment so that you're not too far back, allowing him to cut to the inside, or too close, allowing him to pass you on the outside.

Step-by-Step for Channeling

○ Position yourself to the side where you do not want the attacker to go. Turn sideways, feet roughly parallel to the path of the ball.

○ Use a side step (shuffling run) to retreat with the attacker until you receive defensive support from a teammate.

○ Then apply more pressure to force a turnover.

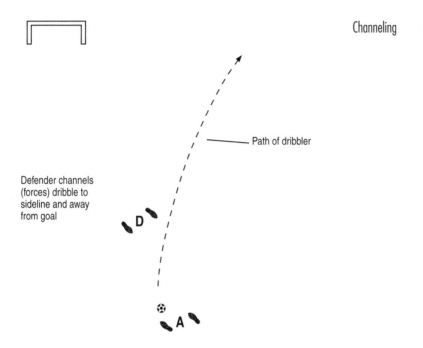

Channeling

Path of dribbler

Defender channels (forces) dribble to sideline and away from goal

Teaching the Offside Trap

An offside trap is a tactic used by defenders to force offensive players deliberately offside. While marking the offensive players, the defenders suddenly move away from the goal as the ball is about to be played, leaving the offensive players in an offside position. This is a tough tactic to master, but if used properly, it is an effective method of frustrating attacks.

Tactical Games

Keep Away—The simple game of keep away in a confined area is a good way to illustrate the fundamental tactics of possession, depth, and mobility. Place three players in a square, 10 yards by 10 yards, and suggest that two of them try to keep the ball from the third. The two with the ball will quickly learn that getting open for a pass is a fundamental tactic. Properly executed, it is very difficult for the lone player to win the ball.

Two versus three players with the ball is even more instructive. Now, defenders have more tactical choices. While one applies pressure on the player with the ball, the other must decide which receiver to cover. If thinking tactically, she will cover the one in the best position to receive a pass. The pressuring player, if thinking tactically, may also be able to apply pressure and cut off a passing channel at the same time. With a larger group, you may enlarge the field of play.

Team in the Middle—This game is similar to "Monkey in the Middle," but with teams. The object is to stay out of the middle; there are no goals.

Divide an area 20 by 30 yards into three equal areas. Mark the areas with cones. Divide players into three equal teams. Put one team into each area.

Give the ball to one of the teams at either end of the field. The two end teams try to play the ball through the middle zone without losing the ball to the team in the middle. Balls may be played on the ground or in the air. Players may not leave their zones during play.

If the middle team wins the ball, it changes places with the team that last played the ball. If an end team plays the ball out of bounds, it exchanges places with the team in the middle.

Encourage players to think about positions, such as keeping some players forward and others back, and passing to where it is easier to send the ball across the middle.

Three-Team Soccer—In this game there are goals, just as in real soccer. Otherwise, the set-up is identical to "Team in the Middle." The object, however, is to stay in the middle of the field. Begin by giving the ball to the team in the middle and allowing the team to choose which end team to attack. The middle team may then enter the end team's zone and try to score a goal. The end team may not, however, enter the middle zone. If the attacking team scores, they may return to the middle and attack the team at the other end. If a defending end team is able to steal the ball and send it into the middle area, it wins and takes over as the middle team. The team that scores the most goals wins.

Once again, encourage players to decide on positions and tactics among themselves.

Multiple Goal Soccer—Use cones to make four or five goals on a field that is appropriately sized for the number and age of your players. Keep the goals small —2 or 3 yards wide—and arrange them randomly and at differing angles. Divide your squad into two teams and tell each to see how many goals they can score. Explain that they can score in any goal and in either direction. The only restriction is that players are not allowed to score through the same goal twice in a row. You may add the further challenge of counting the goal only when a shot passes through a goal *and* is received by a teammate. This game does an excellent job of teaching your players to spread out, to pass, and to communicate.

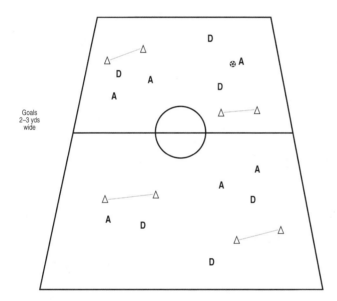

Multiple Goal Soccer

Home Base with a Hornet—As with "Home Base" (described on page 53), mark off a square or circle in the middle of the field or use the center circle of a field. Tell players that this area is the home base or safe area where no one can take the ball from them. Then ask players to leave the playing area (go to the sidelines) and supply each with a ball—except one, who will be the hornet. Tell the players that their job is to get safely to the home base as quickly as possible. Tell the hornet that her job is to slow them down by kicking balls away. This game not only promotes passing, receiving, and communication, but also encourages all manner of creative tactical thinking.

As the group finds ways to "beat" the hornet, add more hornets. Use training vests so players know who the hornets are.

Breakaway!—This is a good tactical game for the whole team, but it is especially good for goalkeepers who want to gain experience handling the inevitable breakaway. Divide the team into attackers, defenders, and goalkeepers. Make one attacker the shooter and line him up about 20 yards from the goal for younger players and 35 yards away for older players. Line up the rest of the attackers and defenders about 10 to 15 yards behind the shooter. On your signal ask the shooter to break for the goal and to try to score. The defenders and attackers pursue and try to stop the goal or assist in scoring. Vary distance between the shooter and the rest of the players to make scoring easier or more difficult.

Space Invaders—This is one of the favorites for many of the teams I have coached. Mark off a field of appropriate size for the age and number of players. Divide your players into two teams. Use training vests. Tell the players on one team that they are defenders and must defend a goal. Line up the attacking team on the sidelines, each with a ball. On your signal have the attackers try to score. This game encourages tactical decision making among both attackers and defenders. For an even greater tactical challenge, tell defenders they must defend both goals. Use a watch to see how long it takes all the balls to be shot into a goal. With accomplished players you may want to stop play after three or four goals. Then have the teams change roles and see how long it takes the new attacking team to shoot in its balls.

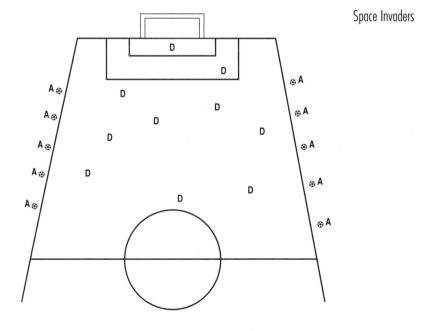

Space Invaders

RULES
OF SOCCER

The rules of soccer have not changed much since they were originally created in 1863. The sport is broken down into seventeen laws, which are discussed here in an abbreviated format. For a complete set of the Laws of the Game, check www.fifa.com on the Internet.

Law 1: The Field of Play—The soccer field is rectangular, with a width of 70 to 80 yards and a length of 110 to 120 yards. The two longer boundary lines are called touchlines. The two shorter lines are called goal lines. A halfway line divides the field equally in two. At each end of the field are a goal area, a penalty area, and a securely anchored goal that is 24 feet wide and 8 feet high. Corner arcs and flag posts are in each corner of the field.

Law 2: The Ball—The ball must be spherical with a circumference of twenty-seven to twenty-eight inches and a weight of fourteen to sixteen ounces. The referee will stop the match to replace a defective ball.

Law 3: The Number of Players—A match is played by two teams of eleven players each, including the goalkeeper. A match may not start if either team has fewer than seven players. Up to three substitutions may be made in an official match. A substitute may only enter the field of play after receiving a signal from the referee.

Law 4: The Players' Equipment—The basic equipment consists of a jersey, shorts, stockings, shin guards, and footwear. The shin guards must be covered entirely by the stockings. Players may not wear anything, such as jewelry, that could be dangerous to themselves or each other. Goalkeepers must wear colors that distinguish them from the other players, the referee, and the assistant referees.

Law 5: The Referee—The referee controls the match and has full authority. Some of the referee's duties include enforcing the Laws of the Game, acting as official timekeeper, stopping the match because of outside interference or a serious injury, ensuring that a bleeding player leaves the field of play, and restarting the match after it has been stopped. The decisions of the referee are final.

Law 6: The Assistant Referees—Two assistant referees indicate when the ball has gone out of bounds; which team is entitled to a corner kick, throw-in, or goal kick; when a player is in an offside position; when a substitution is requested; and when misconduct or anything else has occurred out of the view of the referee.

Law 7: The Duration of the Match—The match lasts two equal periods of forty-five minutes, unless otherwise agreed between the referee and both teams before the start of play. Players are entitled to a halftime interval of no more than fifteen minutes. The referee allows for time lost through substitutions, injuries, or any other cause. Additional time is allowed for a penalty kick to be taken at the end of each half.

Law 8: The Start and Restart of Play—The winner of a coin toss decides which goal it will attack in the first half. The other team takes the kickoff to start the game. Kickoffs are also used to restart play after a goal has been scored. A dropped ball is a way of restarting a match after a temporary stoppage. The referee drops the ball at the site where the play was stopped. The play restarts when the ball touches the ground.

Law 9: The Ball In and Out of Play—The ball is out of play when it has entirely crossed the goal line or touchline on the ground or in the air or when the referee has stopped play. The ball is in play at all other times.

Law 10: The Method of Scoring—A goal is scored when the entire ball crosses the line between the goalposts. The team that scores the most goals wins. If an equal number of goals are scored, the game is a tie. Some matches use overtime to break ties.

Law 11: Offside—A player is in an offside position if he is closer to his opponents' goal than both the ball and two opposing players at the moment the ball is played by a teammate. *Exceptions:* Players are not offside if on their own half of the field or on the opponents' half but either level with the last defender or receiving the ball directly from a goal kick, throw-in, or corner kick. A player is only penalized for being in an offside position if the referee believes the player was gaining an unfair advantage or interfering with play or with an opponent. An indirect free kick is awarded to the opposing team when a player is offside.

Law 12: Fouls and Misconduct—A direct free kick is awarded to the opposing team at the spot of the foul for any of the following offenses:

- Kicking or attempting to kick an opponent
- Tripping or attempting to trip an opponent
- Jumping at an opponent
- Charging an opponent
- Striking or attempting to strike an opponent
- Pushing an opponent
- Making contact with the opponent before touching the ball while attempting to tackle the opponent
- Holding an opponent
- Spitting at an opponent
- Deliberately handling the ball (except for the goalkeeper in the penalty area)

A penalty kick is awarded if any of the previously mentioned offenses are committed by players in their own penalty area.

An indirect free kick is awarded at the spot of the foul for the following offenses:

- Playing in a dangerous manner
- Obstructing an opponent

- O   Preventing the goalkeeper from letting go of the ball
- O   (As goalkeeper) Failing to release the ball within six seconds
- O   (As goalkeeper) Touching the ball with a hand after releasing it and before it's touched by another player
- O   (As goalkeeper) Touching the ball with a hand when receiving it from a teammate's kick
- O   (As goalkeeper) Touching the ball with a hand when receiving it directly from a teammate's throw-in

A caution (yellow card) is issued to a player who commits any of the following offenses:

- O   Unsporting behavior
- O   Dissent by word or action
- O   Persistent infringement of the Laws of the Game
- O   Delay of restart of play
- O   Failure to respect required distance during corner kick or free kick
- O   Entering or reentering field of play without the referee's permission
- O   Leaving the field of play without the referee's permission

An ejection (red card) is issued to a player who commits any of the following offenses:

- O   Serious foul play
- O   Violent conduct
- O   Spitting at any person
- O   Denying a goal-scoring opportunity by deliberately handling the ball
- O   Denying a goal-scoring opportunity by using an offense punishable by a free kick or a penalty kick
- O   Offensive, insulting, or abusive language
- O   A second caution (yellow card)

Law 13: Free Kicks—Free kicks are either direct or indirect. The ball must be stationary when the kick is taken, and the kicker cannot touch the ball a second time until it has touched another player. A direct free kick can be kicked directly into the goal without touching another player first. An indirect free kick must touch another player before it enters the goal. Unless standing on its own goal line between the goalposts, the opposing team must be at least 10 yards away during a free kick. Opponents must be outside the penalty area and at least 10 yards away from players taking a free kick in their own penalty area.

Law 14: The Penalty Kick—A penalty kick is awarded against a team that commits an offense that warrants a direct free kick inside its own penalty area. Additional time is allowed for a penalty kick to be taken at the end of each half or at the end of an extra period. The kick is taken from the penalty spot by a kicker who has been identified by the referee. The goalkeeper must remain on the goal line until the ball is kicked. All other players must stand at least 10 yards from the penalty spot and be outside the penalty area. The kicker may not play the ball a second time until it touches another player.

Law 15: The Throw-in—A throw-in is a method of restarting play when the ball crosses the touchline on the ground or in the air. The opponents of the player who last touched the ball take the throw-in from the point where it crossed the touchline. The ball is in play immediately when it enters the field of play. The thrower may not touch the ball again until it has touched another player. A goal cannot be scored directly from a throw-in.

Law 16: The Goal Kick—The goal kick is a method of restarting play when the ball, last touched by the attacking team, crosses the goal line on the ground or in the air. A defending player kicks the ball from anywhere within the goal area. All opponents must remain outside the penalty area until the ball is in play. The ball is in play when it is beyond the penalty area. The kicker cannot play the ball again until another player touches it. A goal may be scored directly from a goal kick.

Law 17: The Corner Kick—The corner kick is a method of restarting play when the ball, last touched by the defending team, crosses the goal line on the ground or in the air. An attacking player kicks the ball from inside the nearest corner arc. All opponents must remain at least 10 yards from the ball until it is in play. The ball is in play when it is kicked and moves. The kicker cannot play the ball again until another player touches it. A goal may be scored directly from a corner kick.

ORGANIZATIONS

American Youth Soccer Organization (AYSO)
12501 South Isis Avenue
Hawthorne, CA 90250
Phone: 800-USA-AYSO, 310-643-6455
Fax: 310-643-5310
www.soccer.org

AYSO is an independent nationwide organization with a registration of more than 630,000 youth aged four and a half through eighteen. AYSO stresses participation by all its members; its motto is "Everybody plays." Every effort is made to balance teams, so there are fewer lopsided games. AYSO's Very Important Person (VIP) program allows children with Down syndrome, impaired sight or hearing, autism, and similar problems to play. AYSO relies on volunteers at the community level to maintain the programs.

Fédération Internationale de Football Association (FIFA)
P.O. Box 85
8030 Zurich, Switzerland
Phone: 011-411-384-9595
Fax: 011-411-384-9696
www.fifa.com

Founded in 1904, this international governing body of soccer has 204 member nations. FIFA administers and markets all worldwide soccer competitions, including the World Cup, and governs all soccer rule changes.

Major Indoor Soccer League (MISL)

1175 Post Road East
Westport, CT 06880
Phone: 203–222–4900
Fax: 203–221–7300

The top indoor soccer league in the United States, the MISL season runs from October to April. Seven teams will compete in the 2005 to 2006 season.

Major League Soccer (MLS)

110 East 42nd Street, Suite 1000
10th Floor
New York, NY 10017
Phone: 212–450–1200
Fax: 212–450–1325
www.mlsnet.com

MLS is the only Division I professional outdoor league in the United States. Twelve teams participated in the summer league's tenth season in 2005. Teams play thirty-two regular-season games. The playoffs culminate in the MLS Cup, the league's one-game championship.

National Alliance for Youth Sports

2050 Vista Parkway
West Palm Beach, FL 33411
Phone: 800–729–2057, 561–684–1141
Fax: 561–684–2546
www.nays.org

The goal of the National Alliance for Youth Sports is to make sports safe, positive, and fun for America's youth. The nonprofit organization believes that participation in youth sports develops important character traits and values, and that the lives of youths can be positively influenced if the adults caring for them have proper training and information.

National Federation of State High School Associations (NFHS)

P.O. Box 690
Indianapolis, IN 46206
Phone: 317–972–6900
Fax: 317–822–5700
www.nfhs.org

The NFHS is a national service and administration organization of high school athletics. The mission of the NFHS is to serve its members and its related professional groups by providing leadership and national coordination for the administration of interscholastic activities that will enhance the educational experiences of high school students. The NFHS promotes participation and sportsmanship to develop good citizens through interscholastic activities.

National Soccer Coaches Association of America (NSCAA)

6700 Squibb Road
Suite 215
Mission, KS 66202
Phone: 800–458–0678, 913–362–1747
Fax: 913–362–3439
www.nscaa.com

This is the largest single-sport coaching organization in the United States, with more than 15,000 members. Founded in 1941, the NSCAA provides educational clinics, academies, and seminars to youth, high school, college, and pro coaches. It also offers diploma courses in all fifty states. The NSCAA is dedicated to promoting soccer and to the education of coaches.

National Soccer Hall of Fame

18 Stadium Circle
Oneonta, NY 13820
Phone: 607–432–3351
Fax: 607–432–8429
www.soccerhall.org

The National Soccer Hall of Fame, established in 1979, is committed to preserving and promoting the history and sport of soccer in the United States. The Hall of Fame is on the Wright Soccer Campus and it includes the Kicks Zone (an interactive games area), museum (with lots of old pictures, films, and memorabilia), administrative offices, outdoor fields, Kicks Hall of Fame store, and a library. The Hall of Fame is open seven days a week except for major holidays.

Soccer Association for Youth (SAY)
One North Commerce Park Drive
Suite 306-320
Cincinnati, OH 45215
Phone: 800–233–7291, 513–769–3800
Fax: 513–769–0500
www.saysoccer.org

An independent regional youth soccer organization located mainly in the Midwest, SAY's objective is maximum participation with even competition at various age levels. It serves more than 100,000 members and includes players aged four through eighteen. SAY is a national affiliate member of the U.S. Soccer Federation.

Soccer in the Streets (SITS)
2323 Perimeter Park Drive NE
Atlanta, GA 30341
Phone: 678–992–2113
www.sits.org

A national inner-city youth soccer and education program founded in 1989, SITS has implemented programs in more than fifty U.S. cities. It is an independent national organization that creates introductory programs geared toward enhancing self-esteem and life skills, with soccer as its foundation. SITS aims to build leadership in urban youth; its motto is "Let's kick drugs and crime out of our communities."

United Soccer Leagues (USL)
14497 North Dale Mabry Highway
Suite 201
Tampa, FL 33618
Phone: 813–963–3909
Fax: 813–963–3807
www.uslsoccer.com

The teams of the USL serve as a development system for Major League Soccer in the United States, similar to the minor-league system in baseball. The USL consists of the A-League (Division II), D3 Pro League (Division III), Premier Developmental League (amateur), W-League (women), and Y-League (youth).

US Club Soccer

716 8th Avenue North
Myrtle Beach, SC 29577
Phone: 843–429–0006
Fax: 843–626–4681
www.usclubsoccer.com

This is a federation of soccer clubs founded on the belief that competitive teams and elite players need their own organization—and fewer restrictions. Unlike U.S. Youth Soccer, for example, US Club Soccer players are allowed to "play up" in age, and travel permissions are not required to attend events in other states.

U.S. Soccer Federation (USSF)

1801 South Prairie Avenue
Chicago, IL 60616
Phone: 312–808–1300
Fax: 312–808–1301
www.ussoccer.com

As the national governing body of American soccer, U.S. Soccer, which is directly linked to FIFA, has exclusive governing power over most domestic soccer matters. Programs under its umbrella include the administration and marketing of the U.S. national teams (men's, women's, Olympic, and youth), U.S. coaching, and refereeing development.

U.S. Youth Soccer Association (USYSA)

1717 Firman Drive, Suite 900
Richardson, TX 75081
Phone: 800–4–SOCCER, 972–235–4499
Fax: 972–235–4480
www.youthsoccer.org

The largest youth soccer service organization in the nation, with a registration of more than three million players, USYSA develops and administers recreational and competitive programs for kids ages five through
nineteen and also runs the ODP program, which identifies and develops
top youth talent. Fifty-five state associations are directly affiliated with
the USYSA.

RESOURCES

Magazines

Soccer America

P.O. Box 23704
1144 65th Street, Suite F
Oakland, CA 94623
Phone: 510–420–3640; 800-997–6223 to subscribe
Fax: 510–420–3655
Subscription: One year (twenty issues) for $79
www.socceramerica.com

Soccer America is a magazine for soccer fans that focuses on international, professional, and college soccer—the best source for youth tournament and camp listings. A subscription includes the *Soccer America Yellow Pages*, an annual directory of youth organizations, tournaments, camps, products, and more.

Soccer Journal

NSCAA
6700 Squib Road, Suite 215
Mission, KS 66202
Phone: 800–458–0678

Subscription: Free for NSCAA members; youth coach membership is $50

www.nscaa.com

This is the official publication of the National Soccer Coaches Association of America. Filled with technical and tactical articles for high level coaches as well as soccer news, *Soccer Journal* is published eight times a year.

Striker

1115 Broadway, 8th Floor
New York, NY 10010
Phone: 212–807–7100
Fax: 212–620–7787
www.striker-magazine.com

Launched as a quarterly in 2005, *Striker* magazine hopes to succeed where many (*Soccer Jr., Soccer Magazine, Soccer For Kids, Soccer Digest*, to name a few) did not. Look for lots of features about star players and columns with training tips and equipment reviews.

Women's Soccer World Online

1728 Mulberry Street
Montgomery, AL 36106
Phone: 334–263–0080
Single copy: $2.95
Subscription: One year (six issues) for $15
www.womensoccer.com

This online magazine is devoted to worldwide coverage of women's soccer. Offers news about all aspects of the women's game played around the world. Links to *Girls Soccer World*, an online magazine devoted to worldwide coverage of girls' soccer.

World Soccer

King's Reach Tower
Stamford Street
London, England SE1 9LS
Phone: 011–44–181–888–313–5528
Single copy: $5.45

Subscription: One year (thirteen issues) for $81
www.worldsoccer.com

World Soccer provides detailed coverage of foreign leagues, teams, stars, and competitions, with an emphasis on Europe. Good source for rosters, results, and transactions.

Books

All-American Girls: The U.S. Women's National Soccer Team by Marla Miller, 221 pages, $4.99, Pocket Books (1999)

All-American Girls offers loads of facts, quotes, and stories about members of the 1999 Women's World Cup team; gives readers real insight into the personalities of the players.

Cobi Jones Soccer Games by Cobi Jones and Andrew Gutelle, 103 pages, $16.95, Workman Publishing (1998)

This is a nicely designed book of tips on basic skills and fun games to play in the backyard or at the park. Perfect for youth players up to twelve or thirteen years old. The games and the tips are really good. You can tell that Jones—one of soccer's most popular players—was involved in writing the book. It comes with a size 4 practice ball.

The Complete Encyclopedia of Soccer by Keir Radnedge, 647 pages, $39.95, Carlton Books (1999)

This is a definitive reference book with in-depth information on national teams, international tournaments, and club competitions, including biographies of more than 500 of the world's greatest players of all time.

The Game and the Glory (Youth Edition) by Michelle Akers, with Gregg Lewis, 187 pages, $7.99, Zonderkidz (2000)

U.S. Women's National Team veteran Michelle Akers shares the story of her life on and off the soccer field. Includes anecdotes about her teammates, her personal struggles, her battle with a disease, and her faith.

The Girls of Summer: The U.S. Women's Soccer Team and How It Changed the World by Jere Longman, $14, First Perennial (2001)

Tells the story of how the U.S. women's soccer program rose from international obscurity in the mid-1980s to win an epic World Cup battle in 1999.

Goal! The Ultimate Guide for Soccer Moms and Dads by Gloria Averbuch and Ashley Michael Hammond, 224 pages, $15.95, Rodale Press (1999)

One of the best introductions to youth soccer to date, this book covers all the bases in an engaging format. A handy reference long after you've read the book.

Go for the Goal: A Champion's Guide to Winning in Soccer and Life by Mia Hamm, with Aaron Heifetz, 222 pages, $12.95, 1st Quill (2000)

For the fan who can't get enough of Hamm, the number one female player in the world, this is the book. The narrative is in Hamm's voice and is packed with anecdotes about her career, her friendships, and playing tips for young players.

Make Your Move by Alfred Galustian and Charlie Cooke, 100 pages, $12.95, Lyons Press (2005)

Coerver Coaching, the world's number one soccer skills teaching program, shows how to make twenty-six 1 versus 1 moves in step-by-step photos. It also presents exercises that youth coaches can use to teach the moves at practices.

The Peak Performance by Dr. Ronald W. Quinn, 104 pages, $17.45, QSM Consultants, P.O. Box 15176, Cincinnati, OH, 45215; 513–761–6240 (1990)

Quinn, the head coach of the Xavier University women's soccer team, presents sixty-one different soccer games for player development. Includes a number of sample practice planners. This is an important reference for every youth soccer coach.

Play-By-Play Soccer by Lori Coleman, 64 pages, $7.95, LernerSports (2000)

A book for eleven- to fourteen-year-olds who are new to the game or want to improve their skills, it includes lots of color photos and information on rules, positions, skills, tactics, and practice drills.

The Soccer Coaching Bible from the National Soccer Coaches Association of America, 316 pages, $22.95, (2004)

Top college coaches from across the United States, including Anson Dorrance, Tony DiCicco, and Glen Myernick, offer insights on coaching priorities and principles.

Soccer for Dummies by Michael Lewis, 384 pages, $21.99, IDG Books Worldwide (2000)

A comprehensive book for every level of soccer fan, *Soccer for Dummies* covers a wide range of topics, from coaching to stretching to being a spectator of Major League Soccer.

Soccer for Juniors: A Guide for Players, Parents, and Coaches by Robert Pollock, 180 pages, $12.95, Macmillan (1999)

Pollock, a skilled writer who knows his subject matter, has written a very good book for soccer parents and parent-coaches. It includes in-depth explanations of basic skills, rules, and tactics.

Soccer Practice Games: 125 Games for Technique, Training and Tactics by Joe Luxbacher, $15.95, Human Kinetics (2003)

Luxbacher, author of several training guides, offers 125 games to use during youth practices to improve warm-up and conditioning; passing and receiving; dribbling, shielding, and tackling; heading and shooting; tactical training; and goalkeeper training.

Videos and DVDs

The best sources for soccer videos and DVDs are Reedswain and Soccer Learning Systems. (See the following "Catalogs" section.)

All the Goals of the '99 Women's World Cup. All 123 goals of the 1999 Women's World Cup are shown from a number of angles. (video, 53 minutes)

All the Right Moves. A collection of twenty moves are broken down in detail and shown in slow motion and at match speed. Then, watch pros use the moves in actual game footage. (video, 35 minutes)

Champions of the World. Here is complete coverage of the exciting 1999 Women's World Cup, from the opening game to the U.S. penalty-kick victory over China in the final. (video, 60 minutes)

Coaching Goalkeepers. *Goalkeepers* is filled with drills and exercises for ball handling, catching, diving, positioning, shot stopping, angles, throwing, kicking, foot skills, and more. (video, 90 minutes)

FIFA Soccer Fever: The Definitive Guide to the World's Greatest Soccer Moments. A DVD produced to help celebrate FIFA's Centennial, it offers action from all seventeen FIFA World Cups and all four FIFA Women's World Cups, as well as footage from FIFA's Youth and Futsal tournaments. (video, 195 minutes)

How to Coach Young Soccer Players: Fun Games and Basic Skills. This is a good video for parents and novice coaches who want to keep soccer fun for very young players. (video, 60 minutes)

The Master and His Method. Pelé, the greatest soccer player ever, presents a training program that includes ball control, passing, dribbling, trapping, physical conditioning, and more. (video, 60 minutes)

A New Era. International stars and Coerver Coaching youth players from around the world demonstrate more than sixty games and drills in this three-video series; includes methods for individual and team development. (165 minutes)

NSCAA Soccer Tactics: On the Attack and Defending to Win. A two-disk DVD set from National Soccer Coaches Association of America. It features twelve tactical training sessions led by NSCAA National Staff Coaches. Each training session has approximately twenty minutes of instruction and also contains coaching cues. (240 minutes)

Really Bend It Like Beckham: David Beckham's Official Soccer Skills. A two-disk DVD set that uses slow motion to show off Beckham's genius, including space-making skills, turning skill, crossing, and closing down and defending. Also includes an interview and career highlights. (170 minutes)

Training Girls and Women to Win. This is a three-video series by April Heinrichs, the head coach of the U.S. Women's National Team. Technical, tactical, and psychological preparation geared toward the women's game. (215 minutes)

2002 World Cup Highlights. Here is a video of the most exciting plays of the most recent men's World Cup; includes great goals, spectacular saves, and more. (60 minutes)

Catalogs

Big Toe Sports
404 Holtzman Road
Madison, WI 53715
Orders: 800–444–0365
www.bigtoesports.com

Large selection of footwear, authentic jerseys, balls, gloves, goals, referee gear, and more.

Eurosport
431 U.S. Highway 70A East
Hillsborough, NC 27278-9912
Orders: 800–934–3876
Customer Service: 800–487–7253
www.soccer.com

Everything your club or team could possibly need: uniforms, balls, footwear, accessories, and more.

Reedswain
612 Pughtown Road
Spring City, PA 19475
Orders: 800–331–5191
www.reedswain.com

Specializes in books, DVDs, and videos.

Soccer Learning Systems
P.O. Box 277
San Ramon, CA 94583
Orders: 800–762–2376
www.soccervideos.com

Specializes in coaching videos, DVDs, and books.

Soccer Master
14188 Manchester Road
Manchester, MO 63011
Orders: 800–926–9287
www.soccermaster.com

Large selection of items for coaches, players, and teams.

Web Sites

www.fifa.com
The official Web site of the Fédération Internationale de Football Association, the international governing body of soccer, it includes a calendar of events, world rankings, and the complete Laws of the Game.

www.girlsoccerworld.com
This is a site for girls up to the age of eighteen who are interested in soccer as players, fans, referees, or coaches.

www.goal.com
This site provides in-depth coverage of soccer outside the United States and news about thousands of teams, players, and games abroad.

www.mlsnet.com
This is the official Web site of Major League Soccer. News, schedules, scores, stats, video highlights, ticket information, an "MLS for Kids" section, and more.

www.nays.org
This is the official Web site of the National Alliance for Youth Sports, an advocate for safe, positive, and fun youth sports.

www.saysoccer.org
This is the official Web site of the Soccer Association for Youth.

www.soccer.org
The official Web site of the American Youth Soccer Organization, it provides educational information for players, parents, coaches, referees, and instructors.

www.socceramerica.com
The official Web site of *Soccer America* magazine, it includes lots of up-to-date U.S. national-team and pro coverage and also has helpful camp and tournament directories.

www.soccer-camps.com
Information on how to find a camp—or promote your camp if you're running one—can be found here. It includes a state-by-state camp listing.

www.soccerhall.org
The official site of the National Soccer Hall of Fame and Museum, it provides features on the history of soccer and updates about programs and events at the Hall's campus in Oneonta, New York.

www.soccerinfo.com
This is the best Web site for college scores and schedules.

www.soccerpatch.com
Here is a place for players to view, post, and trade patches and pins of their teams, towns, and tournaments.

www.soccertours.com
Comprehensive details on all levels of tours and tournaments from all over the world are provided here.

www.soccertv.com
As "the ultimate guide to televised soccer," it has detailed information on scheduled telecasts of upcoming games.

www.sportsparents.com

Need-to-know information for parents of young athletes—nutrition, psychology, injuries, sportsmanship, equipment, and more—can be found here.

www.ussoccer.com

The official Web site of the U.S. Soccer Federation, it offers complete coverage of all the U.S. national teams, including ticket information.

www.ussoccerplayer.com

A site developed by U.S. national team players, it provides news, articles, games, puzzles, and playing and coaching tips.

www.womensoccer.com

Need information about all aspects of the women's game, immediate game results, in-depth information, current news, TV listings, ticket information, and more? You'll find it all here.

www.youthsoccer.org

This is the official Web site of the U.S. Youth Soccer Association.

GLOSSARY

Advantage Rule—The rule that allows the referee to decide to disregard a foul if stopping play would benefit the team that committed the foul.

Assist—The pass that leads to a goal.

Assistant Referees—Formerly called linesmen. Two subordinate officials in the single-referee format. Assistant referees indicate when a ball has gone out of bounds, indicate which team has possession, signal infractions and offsides, and consult with the referee in situations in which the referee is not certain of what happened.

Bicycle Kick—An acrobatic overhead kick in which the player leaps into the air, with the legs moving as if pedaling a bicycle, and kicks the ball backward over his head. The bicycle kick isn't recommended for young players.

Box—See "Penalty Area."

Cap—An appearance in an international match for one's country.

Chip—A high, lofted pass or shot over an opposing player.

Clear—To kick or head the ball away from the goal area to prevent the attacking team from scoring.

Cleats—Soccer shoes with studs on the bottom of the sole plate.

Corner Kick—An offensive free kick taken from the corner after the ball has been knocked over the goal line by a defender.

Cross—To pass the ball from one side of the field into the middle, usually in front of the goal.

Dangerous Play—Any play—such as raising the leg above waist height (also called high-foot) in order to kick the ball—that could cause injury to another player.

Defender—A player whose primary responsibility is to keep the other team from scoring.

Draw—A game that ends with the score tied.

Dribbling—Using the feet to move the ball along the ground.

End Lines—The boundaries on the ends of the field where each goal is located.

Far Post—The goalpost farthest from the ball.

Field—The playing area. Under international rules, the length (110–120 yards) of the field must be greater than the width (70–80 yards).

FIFA (Fédération Internationale de Football Association)—The world governing body of soccer. FIFA, headquartered in Zurich, Switzerland, stages the World Cup and other major international tournaments.

Fifty-Fifty (50-50) Ball—A ball that is as near to a player of one team as it is to a player of the opposing team.

Flanks (Wings)—The area of the field near the touchline, often used to describe defenders, midfielders, or forwards who play in that area.

Formation—The basic organization of the players at the start of a game, usually expressed by a series of three digits indicating the number of defenders, midfielders, and forwards. (Example: A 4-4-2 formation indicates a team is using four defenders, four midfielders, and two forwards.)

Forward (Striker)—An attacking player whose primary responsibility is to score goals.

Foul (Infraction)—An offense committed when a player breaks one of the rules of the game.

Free Kick—Kick taken to restart play after an infraction, a score, or the ball's going out of bounds over the end line. A direct free kick can result in a goal without requiring the ball to be touched by another player on either team. With an indirect free kick, the ball must first be touched by another player before a goal can be scored.

Goal—The structure, which is 24 feet wide and 8 feet high, at each end of the field through which the ball must pass to score. A goal is scored when the entire ball crosses the goal line, between the goalposts and under the crossbar.

Goal Area—The lined area, 6 yards by 20 yards, in front of the goal where goal kicks are taken.

Goalkeeper (Keeper)—The player who defends the goal, and the only player who may control the ball with any part of the hands or arms (inside the penalty area).

Goal Kick—A kick taken by the defensive team after the ball is last played over the end line by the attacking team.

Golden Goal—A goal scored in sudden-death overtime that wins a game.

Half Volley—A kick taken just after the ball bounces.

Hand Ball—An infraction that is called when a player deliberately touches the ball with a hand or arm.

Hat Trick—Three goals scored in a game by one player.

Head—To clear, pass, or shoot the ball with the forehead.

Injury Time (Stoppage Time)—The time—usually one to four minutes—the referee adds to the end of a half or a game to make up for time lost when the game was paused for injuries or other problems.

Instep—The top of the foot over the arch, used for kicking.

Marking—Closely guarding a specified opponent and being responsible for that player all over the field.

Match—A game.

Midfielder—A player whose primary responsibility is to move the ball from the defenders up to the forwards and to control the middle of the field. Midfielders have attacking and defending roles.

National Team—A team that represents a country in international competition.

Near Post—The goalpost closest to the ball.

Nutmeg—To dribble or shoot the ball between an opponent's legs.

ODP (Olympic Development Program)—A program run by the U.S. Soccer Federation that identifies and trains high-level youth players in order to produce future national-team players.

Offside—An infraction called on an attacking player in the offensive half of the field if, at the moment the ball is played by a teammate, there are not at least two defenders between the player and the goal. Offside is only called when the player in the offside position is interfering with the play or gaining some advantage by being in that position.

Offside Trap—A defensive technique in which players move up quickly to catch their opponents in an offside position.

One-Touch—When a player receives a ball and passes or shoots it with the first touch, without trapping or dribbling it.

Overlap—To make a run past a teammate with the ball to create space for another pass or to distract defenders.

Own Goal—Accidentally kicking, heading, or deflecting a ball into one's own goal.

Penalty—A foul that results in the awarding of a penalty kick.

Penalty Area—The lined area in front of the goal, measuring 18 yards by 44 yards, where the goalkeeper can touch the ball with his hands. Also referred to as the 18-yard box.

Penalty Kick (PK)—A direct free kick taken from a spot 12 yards in front of the goal that occurs when an attacker is fouled in the penalty area.

Penalty Kick Shootout—A series of penalty kicks used to determine the winner after a game has ended in a tie. Five kicks are taken by each team, and the team that scores more goals wins. If the teams are tied after five kicks, the kicks continue until one team has scored more than the other after the same number of kicks.

Pitch—A British term for a soccer field.

Red Card—A card shown to a player by a referee to signal an ejection from the game. The player must leave the field and cannot be replaced. A player receiving a red card may face fines and further suspension.

Referee—The official in charge of the game: enforces the laws, is the official timekeeper, controls all substitutions, calls fouls and may caution or eject players, interprets rules, and makes sure ball and players' equipment conform to the rules.

Save—When the goalkeeper prevents the ball from going into the net.

Score—To make a goal, or the number of goals each team makes in a game.

Serve—To deliver an accurate pass to a teammate in a scoring position.

Shielding—Keeping yourself between the ball and the defender.

Slide Tackle—To leave your feet and slide on the ground in an attempt to win the ball or knock it away from an opponent.

Square Pass—A pass made to a player who is directly to the side of you.

Sweeper—The last player in the defense besides the goalkeeper; responsible for "sweeping" away all the balls that get past the rest of the team.

Tackle—To use one's feet and body to take the ball away from an opponent.

Throw-in—A method of putting the ball back into play after it has gone out of bounds over the touchline.

Touchlines (Sidelines)—The boundaries on the two longer sides of a soccer field.

Trap—To bring the ball under control, usually with the foot, thigh, or chest.

Volley—A kick that is made while the ball is in the air.

Wall—Several players lined up to block a free kick that is taken close enough to the goal to be dangerous.

Wall Pass—Two players bypassing a defender by quickly passing to each other. The receiving player acts like a wall by letting the pass bounce off one foot, directing it into the path of the original passer, who is running behind the defender. Also referred to as a give-and-go pass or a one-two pass.

World Cup—The world championship of soccer; the international tournament featuring the best national teams in the world, held every four years.

Yellow Card—A card shown to a player by the referee to signal a caution for a flagrant infraction. A second yellow card results in the player's being ejected from the game.

INDEX